# LEARNING TO LOOK

# LEARNING TO LOOK

*Dispatches from the Art World*

Alva Noë

# OXFORD
UNIVERSITY PRESS

Oxford University Press is a department of the University of Oxford. It furthers
the University's objective of excellence in research, scholarship, and education
by publishing worldwide. Oxford is a registered trade mark of Oxford University
Press in the UK and certain other countries.

Published in the United States of America by Oxford University Press
198 Madison Avenue, New York, NY 10016, United States of America.

© Oxford University Press 2021

Library of Congress Control Number: 2021013673
ISBN 978-0-19-092821-6

DOI: 10.1093/oso/9780190928216.001.0001

9 8 7 6 5 4 3 2 1

Printed by Sheridan Books, Inc., United States of America

*For Nicole*

# CONTENTS

Part IV    Nature's Art

# PREFACE

Works of art sometimes leave us speechless. But they almost never shut us up. They can't. There's just too much to say. Talking about art doesn't leave things as they are; it changes everything. To look, to think, to say what you see or why you respond as you do—this changes what you see, and it changes your response. The effort and the caring remake us. They remake us in real time as we listen to the song, or examine the painting, or watch the movie.

This is not unique to art, of course. What I have just outlined goes for all experience and is really life's first principle: life is a process of growth and reorganization, a process that commences right when we first act, for we reorganize ourselves and develop in response to the ways what we do changes what we undergo, as Dewey might have said.

But art *aims* at this; there is art so that we may remake ourselves, and also so that we may catch ourselves in the act of this remaking. Art requires creation, even from its beholder.

Yogi Berra was right: you can see a lot by observing. But observation—the effort and the caring—requires thought, attention, focus. It can be play, but it is also work. Art always proposes a task, and the task is neither easy nor quite well enough defined. It is this: to try to perceive, to bring what is there into focus. If you do this, you will find yourself unveiled and, to whatever little extent, put together anew.

The crucial thing to accept is that we don't get all this—the wow, the pleasure, the unveiling, and the reorganization—just for the price of admission. We have to join in, turn on, throw thoughts and reactions at the works themselves, position ourselves to catch them on the rebound, and allow room for emotions, which are not always positive. This is something we typically do with other people in the field cast by our shared responses, words, and argument.

Works of art are strange provocations. Sometimes they offend us; more often they leave us untouched, unaffected, even bored. But this does not get in the way of their value.

The pieces collected here are exercises in giving art, and myself, the time to let something happen; I try to do my work so that art may do its work.

This book is a companion to *Infinite Baseball*, which I published in 2019. Like that book, this one reworks writings published originally between 2010 and 2017 in my weekly column at 13.7: Cosmos and Culture, which was a science and culture website run by National Public Radio.

Most of the short essays were written while I was working on my 2015 book *Strange Tools: Art and Human Nature*, and they flow from the same curiosity that nourished that project. The title is borrowed from Joshua C. Taylor's famous *Learning to Look*, which was the first book about art that I ever read.

# PART I

## Encounters

# SOUP IS AN ANAGRAM OF OPUS

The Andy Warhol exhibition at New York's Museum of Modern Art in 2015 gave visitors, and me, a rare chance to see Warhol's Campbell's soup can paintings. First painted and shown in 1962, in Los Angeles, the thirty-two paintings have seldom been brought together for display. One critic marked the occasion with a short essay entitled "32 Short Thoughts About Andy Warhol's Campbell's Soup Can Paintings at MoMA."[1] He makes good points—thirty-two of them, actually, one for each painting. But one of these points stands out and deserves restating. These are *paintings*. They are manifestly hand-crafted; they are deliciously variable and detailed even as they depict something machine-made and commercial; they invite and repay visual scrutiny.

I spent about two hours in the gallery and found myself thinking a few additional thoughts, which I offer here as addenda to the critic's thirty-two.

1. I rarely go to a museum these days without noticing how few people actually take the trouble to look at, or pay attention to, the art. There's a sort of paradox at work here. If the works are very famous, you can't see them, because you think you know them and can't see past your own

pre-image. If the works are entirely unknown to you, they may not stimulate your curiosity and capture your attention. In both cases, the natural response these days is to snap a picture—of your child in front of the painting, or of yourself, or maybe of the painting itself—and then you move on. In the approximately two hours I spent in the Warhol gallery I can't honestly say that I saw anyone take a serious look at the paintings on exhibition. These works, so plain, so unadorned, so eminently available to the inquiring eye, were also, and for that very reason, entirely concealed from view, right out there in the open.

In *Strange Tools* I argue that works of art are hard to see on purpose.[2] They don't invite you to admire them, or check them out; they challenge you, rather, to *try* to see them when in fact you can't, at least not to begin with. "See me if you can!" says the work of art. "If you dare!" And it isn't easy to do.

I saw this principle in action there with Warhol's Campbell's soup cans: how would you be affected, how would you be remade, if you were to manage to put your camera away, ignore the person you are with, and actually try to see these misleadingly familiar paintings by Andy Warhol?

2. *Soup* is an anagram of *opus*, which is Latin for "work," as in *artwork* or *magnum opus*. That's pretty cool. Writ large on each of the thirty-two paintings, slap bang in the full focus of the visual field, is a word that playfully suggests what is in fact the case: that these are works, hidden in plain sight by the fact that they don't look like works.

3. What do they look like? They aren't pictures *of* anything, really. They're certainly not paintings of actual soup cans. Nor

are they renderings of the label. He worked not from actual cans with actual labels but from promotional materials that Campbell's sent out. In other words, these aren't so much *pictures* of either cans or labels as they are *reproductions* or *copies* of the commercial graphics, blending design and text. What kind of objects are these? These opera kick up this question like so much dust.

4. This explains in part why the resulting images are cartoonish. The label is reproduced—albeit by hand in an evidently awkward and imperfect fashion—and it is present not as part of a can's actual surface, with roundness and three-dimensionality, but as something flat and extended across the page. The fact that the cans' lids and bottoms are also added on, complete with highlights, is somehow jarring and goofy. The perspective isn't quite right. In the finished work, cartoon cans float suspended in an unreal space.

5. Or maybe they are suspended because they are somehow representations not of this or that soup can, or of a kind of Campbell's soup, but because they are a kind of presentation of the *essential* soup can. The handmade quality reads as a kind of confident abbreviation in his rendering of the can labels. Rather than being pictures, they are icons in the traditional sense—that is, clusterings or agglomerations of identifying or defining traits. Now, this would be curious. It suggests that these paintings are asking real questions about *what* they represent. And yet one can only wonder: why does this subject matter warrant this kind of questioning? But then this, again, is a quintessential art moment if ever there was one, comparable to Duchamp's upending of a urinal.

6. Another word writ large across each of these soups—oops, I mean works—is "Condensed." The soups themselves are condensed, of course, but so are the paintings. They condense not the can, not the soup, not the label, but the very concept of all this into a series of icons. These icons show us our own Campbell's canned soup concept in all its thirty-two varieties.

7. An older lady to my right said to her younger companion: "Now, *this* one"—pointing to the chicken noodle—"*this* is the one that *we* always got." She made this statement in a tone of voice suggesting that this painting had a special meaning for her, as if it was really made *for* her, because she, being of an age and having just the distinct personal history that she had, had a history in which this very soup, Campbell's chicken noodle, had played a distinct role. I was struck by how remarkable this was. Somehow Warhol, by painting something so familiar as to be unremarkable, so commonplace as to be truly undeserving of a rendering, ended up making something special in an intimate way to this person. And I was struck that one painting could function so effectively as a bit of playful, ironic, art-world wit and, at the very same time, be so straightforwardly sentimental and affecting.

8. And then there is the sense, as you look at the paintings cast along the wall, that they are like baseball cards or cans themselves that have been painstakingly collected by someone manic, or compulsive, or determined enough to have gone to the trouble of finding them all. So at least part of what is put on display, part of what is exhibited in a condensed form, is this distinctive and recognizable form of collector's mentality. Warhol is putting the human mind, or at least one of its species, on exhibition. It isn't about soup cans. It isn't about pop culture. It is about us.

# 2 | I AM SITTING IN A ROOM

I was at MIT a few years ago, at the Center for Art, Science and Technology, attending a conference where I got to hear Alvin Lucier performing his twentieth-century masterpiece, *I Am Sitting in a Room*. The performer—in this case the composer himself—records his voice making a statement about what he is doing: "I am sitting in this room, the same room you are sitting in. I am recording the sound of my speaking voice. . . ." And so on. This is then played back and recorded again. This new recording is then played back. And recorded again. Each playback sounds like a pretty faithful rendition of what came before.

After about sixteen rounds of this, however, what we are given is sound that bears no recognizable relation to the original utterance. The sounds we hear are not those of a human voice. The words are gone. Even the rhythm is unrecognizable as that of speech. Something familiar has been made strange before our very ears and eyes, simply through the action of copying. The subtle degradations of each recording cycle get compounded in the iteration and reiteration.

It is magical. It is breathtaking. It is heart-stoppingly beautiful.

At the end we must wonder: are we getting a degraded signal, or is the final message a signal imbued with unimagined new content—a disclosure of the room's very own resonant nature, as the artist himself suggests, or of the true essence of sound, or, indeed, of speech?

That's how it is with art. A phenomenon—in this case the basic phenomenon of speaking, expressing meaning in words, and also that of copying or recording what we hear—is laid bare before our eyes. The artist did so much by doing nothing, by letting nothing happen. In one sense, this was a trick. A gimmick. Like the game of telephone. But a trick so straightforward, and so smart, that it rises to the level of the lyrical; it is music.

The composition is also an interesting example of the way technology and art work together. Tape is an old technology. It was not cutting-edge even in 1970, when Lucier first made this work. And yet the work would be impossible without tape recording. In a way, this is a kind of investigation of what tape recording actually is.

# 3 | FORTY SPEAKERS IN A ROOM

In Wim Wenders's wonderful movie *Wings of Desire*, angels hear what a person is thinking and feeling as they hover nearby. As angels move among people, voices come in and out of focus for them.

Janet Cardiff's 2001 art installation *The Forty Part Motet*, which I got to see at the Nelson-Atkins Museum in Kansas City, Missouri, in the winter of 2017, does something similar. You enter the room and you encounter forty speakers, arranged in an oval, playing a recording of the Salisbury Cathedral Choir singing "Spem in alium" (Hope in any other), which was composed by the English composer Thomas Tallis in 1556. The Tallis piece itself is for forty male voices, organized into eight choirs of five singers (bass, baritone, alto, tenor, child soprano). Cardiff has recorded each singer with an individual mic, and each singer's part is played through just one of the speakers (which, in turn, are clumped into eight groups of five speakers).

You could opt to sit in the middle of the room and listen to the wall of sound created by the joint effect of each speaker, but you could also, angel-like, flit about the room, swooping down on this voice or that, causing, through your action, one voice to pop, and another to be drowned out.

In this way the work invites you not only to enjoy the music but also to remix it. It is an opportunity to intrude, harmlessly, into the intimate sphere of each singer. You can get so close that you can hear their imperfections, or idiosyncratic qualities, in ways that get lost when they are subsumed in the whole, and which you could never hear from your seat in the audience of a conventional concert performance.

This slightly voyeuristic, eavesdropping quality is enhanced by the fact that the recording doesn't stop when the singing is over. You can drop in on the different singers as they chitchat and gossip among themselves.

The whole work, which takes about seventeen minutes (fourteen minutes of song and three minutes of chatting), is less an opportunity for deep listening, in my judgment, than it is an opportunity for manipulating sound by moving around. Your body becomes your mixing tool. You listen to speakers, not singers. When you lean in to pay attention, you lean in to a speaker. And the distortions you produce through your own movements are the direct result of the fact that the recording technology had made separate what was, in the making, collective. The work itself becomes a supercharged technical reconstruction of the music.

I found that there was actually something a bit creepy about all this. Robotic speakers go proxy for absent singers; each is roughly the stature of a human being, with a sound box atop a pole torso. Technology intervenes to undo the communion of the actual singers. And while the song is sacred—translated from the Latin: "I have never put my hope in any other but you, O God of Israel"—a museum or gallery is not a sacred space. There was something jarring about the performance of a distinctively spiritual offering in such a secular context.

And then there is the curious fact that the work collects its public in the giant oval formed by the arrangement of speakers, drawing them in; everyone is visible to everyone else. The work makes a spectacle of us. We get to watch as each of us enacts the sound score and explores the structure. The artist has said that the work is "like walking into a piece of music." Only it isn't, not really. It's not the music, but a curious situation in which one has a technologically enhanced freedom to explore oneself and one's relation not only to the musical work but also to sound, and the body, as well as other people.

It is striking that a fair number of visitors to the gallery do not take the opportunity to mix their own song and settle, as it were, for sitting still and listening to the recording of one. A fair number of folks sit themselves down in the middle of the room and, to my surprise, weep. Apparently there was a lot of weeping at the first showing of this artwork at the Cloisters in New York two weeks after the atrocity of 9/11. I get that. But at the museum? Now? Why? Cardiff herself seems to see this as an important part of what she's doing. She writes (quoted on wall text): "People need this emotional release. They need to have this ability to be in the moment and to feel the sense of presence and spirituality that music like this brings."

This has something to do with why the Cloisters, a branch of the Metropolitan Museum of Art dedicated to medieval art, chose to hold an exhibition of *The Forty Part Motet* shortly after 9/11. This was its first-ever showing of a twentieth- or twenty-first century work.

And yet I can't help but think there's something odd here, something that cries out for explanation. When was the last time you encountered lots of people sobbing with emotion at an art museum?

We've already noticed that there is a disconnect between the manifestly sacred character of the music and its high-tech, magnificently non-sacred display in the secular art gallery. Could it be that it is there, in the loss of the spiritual, in the absence of the sacred in our modern lives, that the work acquires its emotional and aesthetic oomph?

# 4 | TWO LEFT HANDS

I had a chance to see Anri Sala's extraordinary *Ravel Ravel Unraveled* again in New York City in the spring of 2016. I had seen it first at the Venice Biennale back in 2013, and I wrote about it in *Strange Tools*.

You can't sum up really good works of art, and I won't try to do that here. But among the themes of this work of video/sound installation were technology and human life.

In the New York version, there are two rooms. In one, you are presented with two videos of two different piano players each playing Ravel's piano concerto for the left hand in D. The camera is tight on the hands; you can't really see the men themselves, you never see their faces, and you don't see the orchestra. The hands are highly expressive, though, and they capture our interest the way faces usually do. This in itself is remarkable and reminds us of something deep about the human ability to recognize mind and intentional action in the world around us. You can't take your eyes off the hands.

The room is filled with a beautiful and *almost* correct-sounding cacophony: two distinct, different performances of the same music, played on top of each other at the same time. What we hear, and what we listen to, is not the piece for left hand that we think we hear; in fact, we get to hear a piece for not one but two left hands. In effect, we hear a raveling of Ravel by Sala.

In this way, different agencies pile up and confuse. The hands of the players act as if they have a mind of their own. There are the players themselves. There's Sala. And of course there is Ravel. But there is the space as well—the gallery space in New York where I sat in the dark, but also the space in which the music was recorded, a space with its own characteristic resonances.

I say the agencies are confused and confusing. Although it is hard to escape the feeling that the hands are thoughtfully making music, it is *very* hard to tell, at least for me, which hands are making which music. Perceiving what the hands are doing, not to mention making sense of what you are hearing—two versions of the same piece of music played at the same time, as if they were one—is challenging.

Which brings us to technology. We are watching and listening to recordings, not performances, and their double play makes it hard to read sound off of movement, as we are normally able to do pretty effortlessly. In this case, what we hear is something of an impossibility: an orchestra accompanying two different soloists simultaneously. It is a techno-perceptual puzzle, and it's exciting.

The video in the next room ratchets up the complexity of Sala's constructed presentation of the concerto. We now encounter a new performer, a woman—the French DJ Chloë—as she works at a deck mixing two LPs corresponding to the two recordings of the distinct performances we have just witnessed in video. She is no longer content to let the inherent discrepancies between the two renditions stand, nor does she aim at putting them together to eliminate the dissonances. She makes new music out of the two recordings—scratching, pushing, stopping, accelerating, and decelerating the records. What a remarkable collaboration! Sala's staging of Chloë's mixing of two left-handed piano players' interpretations of Ravel's concerto! It really is Ravel raveled and unraveled.

Agency—responsible action, but also ability and disability—and the way technology extends, enhances, transforms, and remakes human agency: these are (among) the themes of Sala's captivating installation. I'm not sure whether it is significant that Chloë is female, while all the other protagonists in this intergenerational, cross-media collaboration are male. But it is very striking that she is presented double-handed—that is to say, *intact*, the very master of her technology, with access to and *control* over the music we've been listening to. It is noticeable that in the video she stands before us bathed in light from the lush green gardens beyond the walls as she wields her craft; the pianists were shown to us in the other room in theatrical darkness, disembodied.

Chloë makes art. And like all art everywhere, the raw materials out of which she makes her art is the making activity of other people.

Anri Sala's strange and beautiful performance illuminates art and technology and their place in our active lives.

# 5 | ROCK ART

Kevin Sudeith refers to his rock carvings as petroglyphs. His medium is an ancient, even prehistoric one. And like his prehistoric antecedents, Sudeith makes icons rather than pictures. A striped bass or an astronaut, for example, is presented as freestanding, devoid of context or situation, as a monument to its place in our lives.

There's something straight-shooting and straightforward about Sudeith's work. The figures are intelligible and the sentiments that lie behind them are suitable for children and grandparents— downright patriotic, almost. And there's nothing wrong with that.

But spend a bit more time in the space carved out by Sudeith's work, as I have (both in New York and in Northern California, where I have had occasion to watch the artist at work), and the utterly *post*modern character of his work jumps into focus, as does its bright wit.

I don't mean the obvious cross-up of using ancient means to make icons of contemporary life and culture.

As an example of what I do mean, consider the fact that Sudeith's work not only is site-specific but also makes unusually specific geological and cultural demands. First, you've got to find good boulders in more or less accessible locations. Second, you've got to get permission to make an artwork out of them. The rocks may be on public or private land. Third, what's required is not just permission to make the work but permission to make a work that will take months to complete and so will require the artist's long-term presence on the land and, in effect, in the community.

The very project, then, is a social experiment; the artist works with rock and carving, but he also works with this more immaterial material of delicate social relations and community.

So Sudeith prowls the backroads of America, far from the art world and its glamorous enticements, looking not only for rocks but also for communities that will allow and enable his petroglyphic grindings.

Now the social experiment deepens. Sudeith doesn't just want to make a picture in the rock that will pass the test of time. He works to document things that are of value for the community itself. These are not decorations; these are social interventions and documentations. The striped bass matters to the Nova Scotia fisherfolk whose boulders he has scored.

And then there is the fact of their near permanence. They are not indestructible, but they do stand a reasonable chance of lasting something like the lifetime of a boulder itself, that is to say, a long time, a geologically long stretch of time. They'll be around after we're all dead and long after Leonardo's greatest paintings have peeled and disintegrated.

Time, its different scales, and our nature as creatures of time, are within the scope of Sudeith's project.

By now you may be wondering how he managed to bring his permanent site-specific boulder art to the project room at Mike Weiss's gallery on West 24th Street in Manhattan, where he had the show in 2016 that prompted me to think more carefully about his project.

He didn't. What he displayed in the gallery were prints, or impressions—one of a kind, made using pulp and pigment at the site itself.

There is a certain irony in the fact that it is the very thing-like rock art, in all its heavy material reality, that resists commodification. It is permanently non-portable, after all. Whereas it is the entirely immaterial social-relations aspect of the work that is more adequately captured in the traces and impressions that can be carried away from the remote locations and brought back to Chelsea.

Heidegger contrasted mere things, like a boulder or slab of granite, with what he called equipment, artifacts manufactured by us to serve this or that use. The work of art, he argued, was a kind of hybrid. Like equipment, and unlike granite, it is made, not found; but unlike equipment, and in this respect like granite, the artwork is autonomous of the uses to which we might put it. Heidegger also believed that artworks carry all sorts of invisible meanings and kinds of importance precisely for human beings who live in a cultural world that wouldn't be what it is if not for the existence of art.

Sudeith makes artworks that put us in mind of this hybrid, intermediate status, of the fact that they reside between granite and technology.

My father, who cares a lot about art, asked me not long ago: what is art going to look like in a hundred years?

Who knows?

But in a way the question is misleading. How it looks, whether it is recognizable to us now as art, is beside the point. As I have argued in *Strange Tools*, works of art are not special bits of manufacture; it is rather that manufacture, in the broadest sense of making activities, is special to us. Tools, technologies, dwellings and living spaces, equipment—the stuff we make—organizes us, fixes our habits, and makes us what we are.

*That* is the stuff of art: the conditions of our living. And however much those conditions change, and so however much the look and feel of our art may change, art and its place in our lives remain unchanged. We make art out of life.

This is what Kevin Sudeith is doing. By making art out of stone, he's making art out of life.

# 6 | THE POWER OF PERFORMANCE

In 2010 I attended a symposium organized in connection with an exhibition at the Hayward Gallery in London's Southbank Centre. The exhibition—"Move: Choreographing You"—looked at the way performance and visual art intersect and collaborate. In addition to lectures and panel discussions with artists, choreographers, and philosophers, there were many performances. I want to share some thoughts about one of them.

As the audience entered Queen Elizabeth Hall (right next to the Hayward, also part of the center) to take their seats, the performers were already on the stage. They sat there casually at the edge of the stage, all nine of them, in street dress, watching the public carefully as we filed in, some four hundred people strong. I remember thinking they looked lovely sitting there. They were watching us, for sure. But I had the impression that they couldn't see us in the way you can see a person with whom you are engaged in conversation. They could only inspect or observe us, as if we were the entertainment. Not because they were blinded by the lights; the house lights were on. But because they, or we, were somehow out of reach, we were occupying different spaces. They were on the stage. Or maybe, in a provisional reversal, we were.

Xavier Le Roy, the choreographer, dancer, and artist who headed up the performance collaboration *low pieces* and can be thought of as its author, eventually addressed the audience, saying something like, "We are going to begin now. What we propose is that we spend the next fifteen minutes, all of us, having a conversation. When the time is up, the lighting person will shut off all the lights. It will be dark for a few minutes. Don't be afraid. Then we will go on."

He also explained that there was no use of amplification during the show, so everyone would have to try very hard to make themselves heard.

I have explored (in my book *Out of Our Heads*) the idea that suckling is a primitive form of conversation, and that dancing is one of conversation's most sophisticated varieties. Conversation is not just talking; it is a dynamic of shared attention and listening. Conversation, like suckling, requires that we lock in, hold on, pay attention, and let go. Partners in conversation don't merely talk about a shared topic; they get caught up in the flow of exchange. Tempo, attitude, posture, rhythm—all get coordinated even though no one does the coordinating.

Most striking of all, to converse with someone—face-to-face, over Skype, or on the phone—is to share a situation with them. You can see, or recognize, the person you are talking to. (This explains the unique dangers posed by driving and talking on the phone. Talking on the phone is not so much a distraction as it is a dislocation, a form of tele-transportation.)

Is it possible for nine dancers on a stage to *have a conversation* with an audience of more than four hundred people in a large theater? No. Definitely not. But then that's the point. Failure is sometimes much more interesting than success.

Just as we couldn't really see each other, we couldn't really talk to each other. But we tried. The audience peppered the stage with questions, directed to no one in particular:

"Why do you want to have a conversation?"
"Can we really have a conversation?"
"Where are you from?"
"Why is the piece called *low pieces*?"
"Will this conversation influence the rest of the show that follows?"

Although the questions were directed to none of the performers in particular, I had the impression that they took turns answering.

At one point an audience member in the front row rose and spoke; she was emphatic, but it was impossible to hear her. She then turned around to repeat herself to the entire assembly. "It is very good," she said, in a European accent of some sort, "that they want us to speak without amplification." A performer herself, she explained, she feared that through use of technology she had begun to lose her ability to PROJECT—she almost sang this word—and it was good, she explained, to try to recover this dying skill.

As time passed, the room was flooded with all manner of different emotions. Some people started shouting things out in irritation. Others seemed to be bored. Still others were showing off, trying to introduce just the right bon mots that would, just possibly, ignite the event for everyone, or make its real meaning transparent.

But no conversation. None of the give-and-take and mutual interest that define a conversation. It was more like a break-dancing battle or some kind of showdown. Them versus us. And then each of us alone for himself. It was a little like being at a demonstration—the whole thing seemed on the verge of going wrong. The tension in the room was palpable.

No conversation, but three things happened that were truly remarkable.

Like the actors on the stage, we became careful observers of the others and indeed ourselves. When a person spoke, everybody at least tried to listen. Of course, the room was large, and most voices were soft. So you could practically hear the room bend its ear, its concentration to make out what was being said.

The second remarkable thing was that the whole episode was absorbing. What started out feeling like a trick or gimmick of some sort now felt like a genuine experiment on the very possibility of conversation and the distinct quality of existence inside a theatrical place. It was as if we had been choreographed and we were the performers. We were rapt, still, facing the people watching us from the "stage," and we were engaged in some sort of larger-than-life display of shouting, feeling, shifting attention, nervousness. As a group, we had been somehow activated and set loose.

My friend said it reminded her of a kind of enactment of the dawn of democratic civilization, like that first general assembly—the Althingi, the all-thing—in Iceland more than a thousand years ago, where tribal leaders came together and chose to talk instead of fight. And that struck me as right. It was not ideas that were on display; no arguments were made or positions defended. There was very little *saying*. What we experienced in the theater was a simple, uncontrived, spontaneous group phenomenon. It had to do with politics and power: speakers sought to project their personal power into the situation. And for the most part they—we, I—could not. What we experienced was a kind of political aspiration. And it was *authentic*. We weren't playacting. This was the best way of carrying on that we could muster in that situation. (Is this what contemporary parliamentary discussion is like?)

And then, with a thump, the lights dropped out and we sat in pitch darkness. Xavier Le Roy later explained to the audience that the tumult that ensued was so loud that the actors on the stage could barely hear their own cues. And now, in a way, we come to the punchline. For what happened, now, in the dark, is that people finally, truly began to talk, in small groups, to each other, to the dancers. And it was loud. A proper conversation? No. Not yet. But an eruption of true speech. It was as if, in the dark, we were able to talk, freed from the burden of establishing a new democracy.

I won't discuss the rest of the evening. The work was staggeringly beautiful. And it achieved so much, right at the outset, in creating a situation in which we couldn't converse or even see each other but in which we could reenact our origins. It demonstrated the power of performance, or of art more generally, to open up ideas and allow for knowledge.

# 7 | CHEAP THRILLS AT THE WHITNEY

There are no chairs to rest on in the galleries at the old Whitney Museum of American Art, where the first-ever New York retrospective of the work of Jeff Koons was on display in 2015. There are some benches by the elevators; they are crowded with people studying their iPhones.

Which got me thinking about Steve Jobs versus Jeff Koons.

It doesn't surprise me to learn that they are, or would have been, almost exactly the same age. (Jeff was born in January 1955, Steve in February of the same year.) And in a sense, they are in the same business. They give the people what they want. Shiny, happy, perfect, expensive manufactured goods. They churn it out and we want to own it.

And so it is fitting that exhausted art consumers tumble out of the galleries and take refuge in their own personal shiny, happy, perfect expensive toys.

It's worth noticing that Jeff really does give Steve a run for his money. Sure, lots of people are using their phones in the galleries to photograph the work. But the fact is, the work is riveting and commands their attention; it actually draws people away from their pocket computers. This is not the usual vaguely church-like let's-make-ourselves-endure-the-art-because-it's-edifying crowd. No, these folks are avidly consuming the art, loving it, and curious about it. The art of Jeff Koons draws attention like an issue of *People* magazine. Who doesn't want to look at the shiny, happy, perfect, expensive images? As with *People*, the Koons show puts lots of sex and celebrity on display. And against the background of the details of Koons's failed marriage to the porn icon La Cicciolina, the exhibition even puts the tragic on display. In one gallery we enjoy images of the couple fornicating (porn style). In the next we are allowed to contemplate a giant mountain of Play-Doh (huge, but made of aluminum with the exact look and texture of colored Play-Doh) with which the artist, so the wall text informs us, mourns his loss of custody over their son.

There is much to love, and hate, in both Jobs and Koons.

Who can deny that Jobs has changed the world? He's changed the way we work and the way we play and the place of technology in our lives. But who can be sure these are changes for the good? And what of the pollution and the economic practices that make these shiny, happy, perfect toys possible at all?

As for Koons, well, he is an artist, and artists don't aim to change the world the way manufacturers do. Artists don't make tools; they make opportunities for self-realization and self-reflection and self-understanding. And they make *things* only because things—as the case of Steve Jobs brings out so nicely—play such a big role in our lives. Koons's making practice is astonishing, a feat of engineering that rivals that of Jobs himself. Consider: replicating a little dime-store hollow plastic King Kong in fifteen thousand pounds of granite, or making perfect copies of inflatable pool toys out of aluminum. And each of Koons's pieces comes packaged, as it were, with important questions for us to ask about precisely our feelings about toys, or cheap consumer goods, or luxury, or celebrity, et cetera. Koons attends not only to the material detail but, if you like, to the intellectual detail as well.

And yet for all that this is Smart Art that people actually Want, there is something also a bit revolting about it. Just as there is something a bit disgusting about the way what Steve Jobs makes takes over our lives and regiments us—remember how people used to lean back, arms akimbo, reading the *New York Times*, but now we huddle over the iPad—so I fear that what makes Koons's work so accessible, and so likable, is not its pop engagement with interesting questions but ultimately its too easy availability, its insistence on meeting us where it finds us, and on supplying us with what we (think we) want: false love, shiny, happy kitsch, banality, bad taste.

And yet, that said, I found the exhibition somehow moving. Retrospectives are always touching—a long life, work to show for it, and now to be feted? That's touching, like a fiftieth wedding anniversary party with children and grandchildren and great-grandchildren all around. But I was moved also by the singularity of Koons's ideas—both technical (his interest in surface and methods of production) and conceptual (the place of toys, inflatables, celebrity, consumer culture)—and by the brute fact that that he has found an audience (collectors, institutions) willing to support and fund his personal making mania. Koons's is a success story.

Finally, I am moved by Koons's sincerity. His objects are lovingly conceived and produced with a commitment to value.

But I can't help wondering: wouldn't the world be better off without what both Koons and Jobs have made for us?

# 8 | WHALING WITH TURNER

According to Oscar Wilde, life imitates art. He wrote:

> Where, if not from the Impressionists, do we get those won-
> derful brown fogs that come creeping down our streets,
> blurring the gas-lamps and changing the houses into mon-
> strous shadows? To whom, if not to them and their master,
> do we owe the lovely silver mists that brood over our river,
> and turn to faint forms of fading grace curved bridge and
> swaying barge? The extraordinary change that has taken place
> in the climate of London during the last ten years is entirely
> due to this particular school of Art.[1]

He might have had a painter like Joseph Mallord William
Turner in mind when he wrote these words. Turner's famous
paintings of ships at sea do not merely illustrate their motif; in
their atmospheric and spacious qualities, they can almost be said
to have created it.

But what of his famous quartet of whaling paintings, which
were on display together in 2016 in New York City at the
Metropolitan Museum of Art? Whaling is a beguiling subject.
On the one hand, back in the 1840s, when Turner made these

paintings, whaling was a hugely important industry. Oil harvested from the fat of the animal was big business, and the bones were used for everything from corsets to umbrellas. Whaling touched the lives of everyone. But on the other hand, it was a big business whose work took place not in local factories but far from public view in the most remote places in the world, out in the middle of the ocean. Whaling touched everyone, but it was a rare person indeed who would ever have set eyes on a whale, let alone witnessed the hunt. So it isn't surprising that, according to text from the exhibition at the Met, "whales, and particularly sperm whales, were quasi-mythological creatures. Most people had never seen one of the animals, and existing images and descriptions, even scientific ones, were generally inaccurate."

Turner himself probably never saw a whale or witnessed whaling firsthand. His renderings, therefore, are products of educated fantasy. Which probably explains their near- total lack of legible detail. The wall text says that the pictures document the parts of the whaling work—the whale is hauled alongside, its blubber is cut away, the oil is extracted using heat and then packed away in barrels, and so on. Perhaps an intelligent and well-informed viewer of these paintings can find traces of these doings notated within. But not this viewer. As far as I could tell, the images were devoid of available detail and had little documentary value.

Nor did they succeed, I would venture, even in capturing anything like the physical reality of the whaling experience. These paintings do little to convey the whale's powerful movement, or that of the ever-shifting and terrifying seas themselves; the harpoon-wielding men seem rigid and stick-figure-like. The vantage point taken up in these paintings, it seems to me, is resolutely optical. We encounter no action, only action's image; what we are given are frozen images.

One of the exhibition's preoccupations is with whether Herman Melville saw these paintings and was influenced by them when he wrote *Moby Dick*. We know Melville knew about them; he refers to them. But it is unknown whether he saw them.

If I had to speculate, I'd suggest that Turner's influence on Melville would have been negligible, at least as far as whaling goes. And this is because, when all is said and done, these paintings of Turner's don't really have much to do with whaling. Whaling is confined to the captions. And besides, Melville had been himself a whaler. It's hard to see how a fantasy of the whale hunt by a painter who'd never even seen a whale or the hunt could have made that big an impression, whatever Oscar Wilde may have thought to the contrary. Is an astronaut likely to be that impressed by a Hollywood space flick?

I don't intend for any of this to be a criticism of Turner. Far from it. Turner was no documentarian. The true reality that interests him in these paintings is not so much the economic labors vaguely adumbrated in the lower portions of the canvases but rather the luminous palisades of cloud, mist, sun, and space that tower thickly above them.

In a way, these aren't pictures of anything, and the question of imitation—art imitating life, or life imitating art?—is bypassed. They are autonomous creations of dissociated atmosphere in paint.

# 9 | TAKE MY BREATH AWAY!

I watched *Top Gun* the other night with my kids. I hadn't seen it in years. It's a remarkable film, first released in 1986, with a visually stunning cast—Tom Cruise, Val Kilmer, Tom Skerritt, Kelly McGillis, and Meg Ryan, among others—and it only gets better with time.

*Top Gun* is a dangerous movie. It aestheticizes killing machines and invites us to get caught up in Cold War jingoism. It's a celebration of a kind of all-male, hungry, competitive, perhaps misogynistic world of warriors in the locker room and the cockpit.

It's also a sexy film where beautiful men snarl and glare at each other in what felt like displays of erotic desire only masquerading as a drive for dominance.

But more than anything else, it is a work of dazzling filmic choreography. George Balanchine has nothing on Tony Scott's exhibition of counterpoint and organization as men and fighter planes maneuver on the deck of an aircraft carrier, eventually upswelling into a gravity-defying, soaring supersonic pas de deux of jets in flight, all to the thrilling pulse of Kenny Loggins's soundtrack-defining song "Danger Zone."

The movie is an extended rock video, a dance-on-film put together from imagery of men in uniforms and planes moving impossibly through and around and astride the painted sky.

The timing and repetition reminded me of the opening scenes of what I had always thought of as an incomparably greater film: *Alien*, the creation of Tony Scott's brother Ridley. That movie opens with an alternative vision of human/machine ballet—the whir of technology as the ship's computer ("Mother") wakes her crew ahead of what turns out to be a deadly encounter with a beast who has come to turn every person on the ship into a host for alien offspring.

*Alien* is blanketed in the dark silence of space. But it is also a composition of movement and sound, an unfolding dance between human beings, their machines, and an alien with fertile and violent impulses. As in the case of *Top Gun*, the action happens in the hot, closed confines of spaces that have been designed by distant governments or corporations for obscure ends that finally mean little to the people sweating it out onstage.

Take a look at *Top Gun* again. It will take your breath away!

# 10 | SPEAK, DRAW, DANCE

A snail moves down the garden path and leaves a trail of ooze behind it. It leaves its mark. So begins the natural history of drawing.

To draw is to make marks, and marks are—certainly before the age of printing and the computer—always the traces of movement, or action. Writing, we forget, is a species of drawing, not a species of talking. In our culture we tend—usually unwittingly—to think of talking on the model of writing: we take ourselves to be stringing together sounds to form linear progressions of words. We forget that talking is a strange ballet we undertake with tongue, lips, throat, eyes, and hands. Talking is like dancing, and writing— well, writing is a way of making traces; it is a kind of drawing. (In Old English, *writan* meant "to score, outline, draw the figure of.")

Anne Teresa De Keersmaeker's performance of an excerpt from her work *Fase* at the Museum of Modern Art in New York in 2011 as part of the exhibition "On Line: Drawing Through the Twentieth Century" combined all these ideas and much more. Seen from above, and as captured in photographs by Thierry de Mey, the dancer's movements disturb the sand floor. As she steps, she draws, she writes, she dances, and she sings.

# 11 | BEACH BEASTS ON THE MOVE

If you know Theo Jansen's strandbeests, then you surely have in mind images of mammoth artificial creatures—made of PVC, plastic ties, bottles, and other elements—roaming the northern beaches of the Netherlands, on the watch for rising seas. The strandbeests are like Patrol Cats guarding the shores, right out of *The King's Stilts* by Dr. Seuss.

Theo Jansen, the artist, writes on his website that he is occupied with creating new forms of life:

> Not pollen or seeds but *plastic yellow tubes* are used as the basic material of this new nature. I make skeletons that are able to *walk on the wind*, so they don't have to eat. . . . [E]ventually I want to put these animals out in herds on the beaches, so they will *live their own lives*.

PVC-based life? Somehow the idea seems less crazy when you actually see his creations at work. Of course, it is one matter to make something that resembles the action or behavior of living beings. It's actually not that hard to do that. It seems to belong to our nature to see personality and life all around us, even in rag dolls and smiley faces. But it is another matter entirely to create something that is truly alive.

Looking at Jansen's handiwork reminded me of Karl Sims's marvelous digital simulations of natural evolution from back in the mid-1990s.

What is life? When would it be right to say that Jansen's or Sims's creatures are alive? Jansen's intuition is that life is tied to problem-solving, to coping with basic tasks necessary for survival. In the case of the beach beasts, this means letting the winds carry you along without being destroyed by their forces, navigating the shore without getting sucked into the water. Every change Jansen introduces to their design and function is a direct response to these real survival challenges. The result of this evolutionary process is, or would finally be, autonomy.

Is it right that life is tied in this way to autonomy and problem-solving, to self-sustaining activity? Are living beings just machines that, within limits, can keep themselves up and running? Is the difference between Jansen's strandbeests as they exist today and their descendants that might someday patrol the coasts of Holland just a matter of degree? Or is life *qualitatively* different? These are the questions Jansen's art brings out of hiding.

We are afforded a very different angle on Jansen's creatures at the exhibition "Strandbeest: The Dream Machines of Theo Jansen," which was up at San Francisco's Exploratorium in 2016. The only live specimens you'll get to see are tame, domestic cousins of the beach-dwelling giants, powered not by the waters and the winds but by compressed air. And most of what is on exhibition are members of lines of the strandbeest genus that are now *extinct*.

Not that it is any less impressive for all that. To enter the great space of Pier 15 along San Francisco's Embarcadero, where the beast remnants were on display, is breath-stopping and awesome. I was reminded of what it's like to enter the great hall of the Museum of Natural History in New York and come across the giant blue whale suspended beneath the ceiling.

Indeed, Jansen's animals *are* awe-inspiring works of human artifice. But that isn't how they read. Nothing is arbitrary here. These may be literally the handiwork of the physicist-turned-artist Theo Jansen—there's a nice film in the show (*Strandbeesten* by Alexander Schlichter) where you get to see him heating and bending and cutting and blowing life into his pseudo-life-forms—but there is no whim, no fancy, no play at work here. Only a single-minded commitment to letting the demands of *survival* in the blustery conditions of the open coast dictate form and structure. Jansen is a proxy here for nature itself, or for Darwinian algorithms of change, even if he is also at the same time *the creator*, in the fullest sense.

The theme of extinction is not lost on Jansen, or on the curators of this excellent exhibition (led by Marina McDougall, whose project it was to bring strandbeests to the Exploratorium). One wall of the gallery displays beast "fossils"; the PVC hangs on the walls, parched, bone-like, dead, labeled. Another wall displays the organization of the various strandbeest clades or lineages.

The show is a joyful one. You can't look up at the skeleton-like remains without feeling something like reverence. This is not art. This is not science. This is life—and it commands our attention in the way that only life can. Or, rather, in this case, an imagined fantasy of whole races of creatures come into being and now gone extinct.

"Jansen's work inspires new reverence for the rarity, the preciousness of life, as well as the tragedy of any species going extinct—given the eons it takes for nature to make a stick insect, a pelican, or an octopus," as MacDougall explained to me by email.

I woke up one morning recently to the dreadful news that we are losing the elephants of Africa. I was reminded of words uttered not long ago by a close friend: *I do not want to live in a world without elephants.*

I do not want to live in a world without elephants. But I am grateful to live in a world that makes strandbeests possible.

# 12 | MAKING THE WORK WORK

An article in the *New York Times* some time ago highlighted the concern of museum curators and event planners with finding ways to make works of art accessible to the viewing public.

The director of Harvard's Peabody Museum has turned to brain science for clues to the way art manages—or, as is often the case, fails to manage—to ignite the imagination and pleasure centers of the viewing public.

In my judgment, the turn to neuroscience is an abdication of the museum's real mission, which is not to cause this or that to happen in the brains of unsuspecting visitors but rather to afford motivated, interested, curious individuals the opportunity to appreciate what is on display. Which is not to say that this is an easy task.

How many times have you entered a gallery in a museum and just, well, kept on going, more intent on wending your way to the museum's end station (the cafe! the bookstore!) than on engaging in the hard work of getting to know—really perceiving—art along the way?

After *Strange Tools* came out at the end of 2015, I had a chance to meet art museum people around the world. Again and again, I listened while they voiced this concern: how to make the work

*work* for people of different backgrounds, different knowledge, different motivations.

Institutions make different decisions. The San Francisco Museum of Modern Art, for example, has turned to new digital, GPS-empowered technologies to provide app-based experiences of the museum's materials. The app knows where you are and what there is to see—and offers you text, video, and narrative to help you. (I was actually invited by SFMOMA to work on this project.) Other museums, such as the Met in New York City and London's Tate, also are exploring the use of apps to go beyond the traditional audio guide.

I thought about all this as I visited the Matisse/Diebenkorn exhibition that was on view at SFMOMA in 2017. The show was fascinating. Henri Matisse is a familiar giant, one of the cardinal points on our art compass. The striking thing is that Richard Diebenkorn, who grew up in San Francisco, shines by comparison, at least in the context of this exhibition. Matisse seems classical—but also staid and interior, dark and a bit voyeuristic—beside Diebenkorn's giant, outdoor, sunlight-filled paint spaces.

The logic of the comparison is compelling. Matisse was one of Diebenkorn's heroes; Diebenkorn's encounters with the senior artist's work made an impression not only in the younger artist's rumination but also in the work itself. For example, when Diebenkorn turned to representation in 1955, not long after seeing a show of Matisse's work in Los Angeles, it must have seemed obvious that Matisse was exerting an influence. Color combinations, scale, and choice of subject matter seemed to be taken over from Matisse.

Not that anyone would ever mistake a Diebenkorn for a Matisse.

The decision to frame Diebenkorn's large, generous, free, spacious works as in dialog with Matisse's very different, European painting was one of the curatorial decisions made to deal with the basic question with which I began: how do you give an audience a leg up on the interpretive challenge of making sense of painting?

Diebenkorn was an educated painter, and his interest in—and response to—Matisse is well documented. Still, there's something arbitrary and gimmicky about the pairing. The story of Matisse's influence on Diebenkorn is never more than a good story, a hook to keep a viewing public interested until they can find a way to actually notice or be gripped by the work itself.

In fairness, it may be that a good story, a gimmick, is just what any presenter requires to enable a visitor to unwind, open up, and gear into art.

# 13 | IRRATIONAL MAN

Woody Allen's *Irrational Man* tells the story of an alcoholic philosophy professor, played by Joaquin Phoenix, who arrives one summer to take up a teaching gig at an idyllic, elite liberal arts college.

I'm not sure what is more far-fetched, the proposition that the entire campus is aflutter with erotic anticipation at the "brilliant" man's arrival or the idea that Joaquin Phoenix is supposed to be a brilliant philosophy professor.

In any case, appearance and reality are at odds in this story from the very start. Professor Abe Lucas is brilliant! This is repeated by different characters like a mantra throughout the movie. But he isn't really. He also is the object of sexual fantasy and gossip across the campus; yet, as we learn soon enough, he's "lost the zest for life," euphemistically speaking. Although he may stand for philosophy in this philosophical movie, it gradually becomes clear that he is not philosophy's voice.

What sets appearance and reality against each other here is fantasy. Jill (Emma Stone), a philosophy student, is (somewhat preposterously, perhaps) fascinated by Abe Lucas, or by the idea she has of him and his adventurous, brilliant past; she has a fantasy about what a life in philosophy can be. That's fine and good—she is a student, after all.

Rita (Parker Posey), his colleague in the chemistry department, is a horse of a different color. She framed a desire to leave her job and husband and run away to Spain with Lucas even before she laid eyes on him, before she came to know him in either a platonic or a biblical sense. Neither his subsequent inability to perform sexually, at the beginning at least, nor the dawning possibility that he might be a murderer, does anything to diminish her desire.

But it is Lucas the philosopher who reveals himself to be most in the thrall of a false picture, not only of the world around him but also of himself.

The movie's key scene is when he and Jill eavesdrop on a conversation at the next table in a restaurant. They learn about a corrupt judge who is abusing his seat and hurting innocent people. In a flash, he forms the intention to murder this judge.

Lucas articulates his reasons: "The judge is a bad man. . . . The world would be a better place without him." But these reasons are ridiculous and impotent—at best rationalizations. He knows nothing about the judge or the people he overhears. The basic truth here is that Lucas wants to kill. And he lies to himself about why. But the resolution to do so immediately delivers him rewards. It turns his life around. He stops drinking and he recovers an appetite for food—and also for women. He likes the idea of himself as a philosophical avenger, a "dark knight" of morality.

Earlier he had explained to his class that Kant was wrong, the ends do justify the means. And anyway, he insisted, in the real world people just act. Reasons, justification, philosophy—these are just talk.

Neither Lucas nor the film does anything to establish these strong claims. But there's no doubt about the fact that talk is the best that Lucas has to offer. He is no lover of knowledge, no philosopher, really, not any more than Rita is a true lover of him.

In the end it is only Jill, the student, who genuinely opts for knowledge over fantasy. When she realizes that her professor is a killer, when she grasps the utter irrationality of his actions and the poverty of his self-image, she finds him repellent. She really sees him and admits to herself what she sees. And what she sees disgusts her.

When she confronts him, she is angry, in shock, horrified. She knows what he has done is wrong. It is obvious. The idea that there is any justification for what he has done is absurd. But she can't justify herself; she feels she can't find the words. She's no match for him intellectually, she says. "He's too brilliant!"

This is where the philosophy happens in this movie. We encounter here an opposition not just between Lucas and Jill but also between reason-based argument and gut feeling. But, even more interestingly, this opposition is immediately shown to be, in a way, a false one. For one thing, as we have seen, he is moved by gut feelings no less than she. Nobody really does anything for a reason in this movie.

But at the same time, whatever she may say to the contrary, she does give reasons and arguments; moreover, she, like Lucas and all of us, recognizes that we can't ever evade the question of reason. We can always ask, "Why?" And we can legitimately demand justification, of ourselves and of others.

Thought and feeling are not opposed to each other; they work in tandem in our lives.

Now *that* is a philosophical lesson, or upshot. It's not Jill's, or Rita's, or Lucas's. It's not something that any of them say. I said that Lucas is not philosophy's voice in this film. It is the film itself, the work of art itself, that engages with these questions.

One of the charms of Allen's movies is the way he puts people on display in what they say. His movies are driven by conversation. In his enacted conversations, we get to see not only what people think about themselves as well as about each other but also how they choose to show themselves in their social worlds. *Irrational Man* is no different. But much of the conversation in this movie is philosophical; it is quasi-Socratic dialogue, and what is enacted are arguments and justifications for our actions. Do ends justify means? Are we free to do what we want? Are we free to act according to our own, perhaps entirely individual, conception of what is right?

Much of what gets illuminated in Allen's cinematic conversations—as in the conversations of a genuine philosophical dialog—is never said aloud and perhaps cannot be made explicit.

# 14 | *ROBOCOP'S PHILOSOPHERS*

I went with my colleague Hubert Dreyfus to see the remake of the movie *RoboCop* when it came out. As it happens, the movie features a character named Hubert Dreyfus. The character in the movie isn't based on Professor Dreyfus; it is an homage to him.

Dreyfus-in-the-movie is a senator who's bent on protecting the people of America from the dangers posed by robot police drones. Like his namesake, Senator Dreyfus is against the robots. The real Professor Dreyfus, who died in April 2017, was famous for his criticism of AI. He was the author of What Computers Can't Do, as well as the equally influential What Computers Still Can't Do. Dreyfus believed that AI rests on a mistake. People are not robots and our lives aren't grounded on rational computation. We live in a landscape of values; things matter to us, have saliences, capture our attention and our concern. We aren't detached the way we would be if we were purely rational. We are not natural-born robots.

Senator Dreyfus and the movie's creators don't do a very good job presenting the philosopher's position. But they get its basic upshot right. We can't trust robots with life-and-death decisions. They lack the wisdom to make hard choices. They've got no feeling. Professor Dreyfus would have added that powers of reasoning and online access to all the information in the world won't help. For there are no algorithms for dealing with the hard cases. This is something that wise people understand. To be a good judge is not to apply rules blindly. It is to make hard decisions in the absence of rules that tell us how to act.

If Senator Dreyfus stands for skepticism about the limits of AI, Dennett Norton, the film's brilliant engineer, represents not only the hypothesis that all there is to being human is information processing but, further, an optimistic commitment to the value of research and the power of technology to make the world a better place. Like his namesake, Daniel Dennett, who has elaborated and defended the prospects of artificial intelligence more profoundly than anyone else, Dennett Norton is a progressive, one of the good guys; he'd rather be enabling amputee guitarists to play again than designing weaponized drones.

It's difficult to find an argument for one side or the other in *RoboCop*. On the surface the movie seems to buy into an opposition between the rational mind and the emotional soul; the latter makes humans special, whereas the former is shared by human and machine. Neither Dennett nor Dreyfus would have much truck with that opposition, though.

But it is possible to read the movie as pulling the rug out from under that simple-minded opposition. Alex, the hero robot cop, comes out of the lab an unfeeling drone, acting automatically, according to program. But gradually he takes form as a person with values, memories, projects, and feelings.

Now, you could read that as endorsing, in a somewhat mystical way, the idea that the human soul triumphs in the end; after all, Alex was once a healthy, living human being.

But there is a better way to understand the story. It offers a rec-onciliation of Dennett's and Dreyfus's views.

Dreyfus was right all along that you don't get a mind out of a computer program; insofar as Alex is just a computer, then, to that extent, he's just a machine.

But Dennett is right too. A robot isn't just a computer. Alex has a body, and he faces problems; he is thrown into the world. His internal states have meaning not only in virtue of the program-ming but also in virtue of the way the robot and the world get tied together.

This is a paradoxical upshot, but a surprisingly plausible one.

It does justice to the idea that even if we are just machines, we aren't *just* machines. A person is a locus of engagement with the world. And after all, if there's one thing we know, it's that, well, we are just machines, but we aren't *just* machines!

This means that artificial intelligence, even if it is successful, doesn't solve the mind-body problem. Just because we make it doesn't mean we understand it.

Perhaps the film's real focus, like that of the original of which it is a remake, is the criticism of corporate capitalism. OmniCorp, the corporation behind the weaponized drones, isn't interested in doing good or keeping the peace. It seeks market domination. And so the movie makes the argument that there are dangers attached to technology whatever stand we take on the more philosophical problems, especially in the setting of capitalism.

This movie's clear villain is Raymond Sellars, the leader of OmniCorp and the one behind its inhuman handling of milita-rized AI. He's evil and he's a crook.

Now here's our question, mine and Dreyfus's: why is the baddie named Sellars?

Wilfrid Sellars is one of the giants of twentieth-century American philosophy.

Can it be a coincidence that Dreyfus and Dennett face off in *RoboCop* against a bad guy bearing the name of yet another noted philosopher?

Yet neither the real Bert Dreyfus nor I, philosophy professors both, nor the friends and students who joined us that day at the movies could come up with a plausible link between the movie Sellars's villainy and the work of the great philosopher of the same name.

Any ideas?

# 15 | POINTING THE WAY TO LIBERATION IN *STAR TREK: VOYAGER*

I grew up with *Star Trek* reruns, and I was an enthusiastic viewer of *The Next Generation* and also *Deep Space Nine*. But somehow I had missed *Star Trek: Voyager*. Until a couple of years ago, when I started working through the seven-year series on the internet.

It's good, and different from the other *Star Trek*s. Until recently, anyway, the franchise has always been a fantasy about a better future, with clean technology and human rights and food replicators and the health and wealth and moral vision to explore strange new worlds in a search for knowledge. But it's also always been a vision of a future in which our lives are structured in almost military-like power hierarchies.

*Voyager* breaks with all that, or tries to. The crew of the *Voyager* has been transported to the far reaches of the galaxy. They know where they are. But they have no way home. Or rather, it will take their whole lives to make it back. And, crucially, they have no way to communicate with home. The crew knows that they will be counted for dead, presumed lost, and that friends, family, and lovers back home will move on with their lives. The crew of *Voyager* is utterly and truly alone. They are disconnected from the people and institutions that are the normal background of our lives.

The only thing still linking the crew to home is their hope that one day they will return.

And so I was startled when, in the middle of season four, they are able to establish a communication link to home. "You are no longer alone," comes a message from Star Fleet Command. "We will not ever give up on you." And gradually a trickle of letters from loved ones begin to reach the crew of *Voyager*.

It turns out the link—an accident of alien technology—is short-lived, and before long *Voyager* is on its own again.

But with what a difference!

They are still a lifetime away. But they are on the books again. There are people waiting for them. Pension funds are reactivated, presumably. "Dear John" letters have been sent and received. Life goes on aboard *Voyager* just as before, though now with a completely different character. As the message put it, they are no longer alone. However far away in space and time, they are back in the embrace of civilization.

"Oh no!" I groaned.

As viewers of *Star Trek: Voyager*, we had grieved for the crew's loss, their isolation, their existential predicament. But we also experienced their situation at some level as their liberation, freed from the control of background, family, and career. To be free of the responsibility of getting innumerable messages that need answering!

The puzzle at the heart of *Star Trek: Voyager* is that the crew is cast away, lost in space, and so they are not so much set adrift as set free. As the messages from home start flowing in, I found myself fearing for the crew. To hear from loved ones and employers, to find out the news of home, was to be found, to be captured.

This is a theme that's been on my mind a lot lately. I wonder if I would have viewed these episodes differently had I watched them back in the late nineties, before the age of twenty-four-hour email-social media-multimedia work/play ensnarement that characterizes life today.

A colleague of mine not too long ago posted a desperate plea online: how to deal with being inundated by email? Too many messages—too many important, worthwhile messages—to answer. She put out the call: *Help! What's a good strategy for coping? Voyager* crossed my mind.

I had similar thoughts in connection with Malaysian Airlines 370 which went missing, tragically, and terrifyingly, in March 2014. In the early days, when there was speculation about what might have happened to the plane, I found myself privately fantasizing that maybe the passengers and crew of the plane had just absconded, freed themselves of life's incessant pressures and paralyzing entanglements and escaped to a tropical island. A large-scale conspiracy to get some peace!

I realize this is a cruel idea and I don't for a second want to minimize the terrible loss of life and the suffering of survivors. But the constant coverage of their loss, in the absence of any information about where they'd gone to, kept driving this thought into my head: the thought that we are overburdened and trapped through our own connectivity.

Death is not the liberation any of us would choose. Some of us might opt for life aboard *Voyager*, though, if given the chance. But all of us, surely, need help balancing the complicated demands of life in the information age.

You don't need to be antisocial or irresponsible to wonder if it might be possible to truly log out, just for a while.

# 16 | AN AWKWARD SYNTHESIS

The Pixar animatied film *Inside Out*, directed by Pete Docter, is the playful and ambitious story of the emotional life of a young girl, Riley, who is uprooted when her parents move to a new city so that her father can take up a job. Like a lot of science fiction, the fiction drags because the science never really makes any sense. Riley herself never comes into focus as a person; her parents, teacher, schoolmates, past life, and new environment are sketched in the most generic terms.

In a way, that's the movie's point. Life's true dramas, it is implied, are internal, and there's little more to Dad or Mom or place than the role these play in triggering events inside Riley or inside each of us. And that, I think, is where the movie falls flat. It purports to be the story of a girl, but in fact there is no girl character in the film. Riley is more like a robot, than a person, that is, she is a vessel whose actions and intentions are controlled by would-be persons—emotion and memory workers—inside her. Riley is no more an agent in her own right than, say, a ship is an agent in its own right. Like a puppet controlled by the team working in head-quarters, *she* is empty.

Descartes (1596–1650) offered, but did not endorse, the idea that the body is a ship and the self resides in the body the way a ship's pilot does. Hume (1711–1776) advanced the idea that there is no self, that what we call the self is in fact just a bundle of perceptions, feelings, ideas. Contemporary cognitive science combines these two ideas in a most awkward synthesis: we are our brain, which in turn is modeled not as *a* self but as a vast army of little selves, or agencies, whose collective operations give rise to what looks, from the outside, like a single person or animal; but, the awkward synthesis continues, some of the events happening inside of us really are *ours*, they really are *experienced*, and this is because they happen in a special way or in a special place, in what the philosopher Daniel Dennett has called the Cartesian theater.

*Inside Out* begins with a question, posed by the movie's narrator, Joy, who is an emotion living inside Riley: did you ever look at a baby or a person and ask yourself, *What's going on in there?* A good question, but the movie's playful answer unfolds more like a textbook presentation of the awkward synthesis than like any kind of insight into what it is like to be Riley or any other person. Headquarters is staffed by five emotions (Joy, Sadness, Anger, Fear, and Disgust). These compete among themselves to operate the joysticks and dashboard that control the person whose emotions they are. They handle, store, protect, and discard experiences; at night they do Dream Duty, projecting film clips (memories) onto the screen of Riley's consciousness. Each of them, driven by their own dominant disposition—Sadness tends to be sad, Joy tends to be optimistic and happy—participates in a kind of give-and-take, a negotiated peace in which they manage Riley's states and cause her to react to events in the world around her.

My ten-year-old son turned to me during the movie and asked whether the brain people in Riley's head had brain people inside their heads too. And later on, showing even more insight, he suggested that the problem with the movie was that nothing much happened.

*Exactly.*

The homuncular model of the brain or mind is something we've dreamed up to help us make sense of the fact that we, ourselves, feel and think and value; we perceive and we act. The fact that our ability to do all this depends on what is inside us shouldn't be taken as an excuse for believing that we, and the things we love and value, loathe and fear, are really just inside us. Or that our engagement with the world around us is nothing more than the upshot of actions undertaken by puppeteers or emotional engineers within.

I'm surprised that Docter and the brilliant creators at Pixar don't appreciate that there is something downright terrifying about this nihilistic conception of ourselves as zombie puppets living in a confabulated universe.

I don't mean to be humorless about this. I get the joke. It's an old one. Recall the sperm people in Woody Allen's *Everything You Always Wanted to Know About Sex* who live and die by the motto "Fertilize an ovum or die trying!" Or the Taste Buds in the 1979 Budweiser commercial who complain about the dry mouth that accompanies the munchies.

My complaint, really, is the humorlessness of Docter's treatment of the idea in *Inside Out*. It's as if he doesn't realize this is a joke. The story is told as if we are really getting inside a person. At best we are getting inside a cartoon not of the person but of her brain.

A final note on gender: Pixar, like Disney, has tended until fairly recently to be a boys' world. The films have had mostly male characters and have been made mostly by men. *Inside Out,* which was released in 2015, marked something of a new beginning. And so it is significant that the main character is an ice hockey player; girls play ice hockey too. And yet, insofar as Riley never comes into focus as a true flesh-and-blood girl, there is something odd about the fact that Riley (isn't Riley a boy's name?) plays a stereotypical male sport (ice hockey). It's as if the film's creators resist really dealing with a female character. Although Riley and her mother are certainly called on to play the stereotypically feminine role of supporting Dad as *he* settles into the new job for which they accompanied him to San Francisco. And it's hard to know what to make of the fact that Riley's emotion controllers consist of three females in dresses (Joy, Sadness, and Disgust) and two men in male garb (Fear and Anger). Are fear and anger *male* emotions? Are disgust, joy, and sadness female? And then there's the fact that Riley is the only character we meet whose internal chorus is made up of male *and* female characters. Mom is all female within. And Dad is all male. Is Riley bisexual because she's prepubescent? Is there a biological theory of gender at work here? (It would be interesting to ask: how would race fit into these picture? In what sense might these defining homunculi have race, or might there be internal variation in the race of one's internal agencies? If these questions make little sense, this is because the whole homuncular picture is so simple-minded.)

If you measure the success of a movie not so much by how entertaining and truthful it is but rather by the opportunity for energetic critical thinking that it affords, then *Inside Out* is a successful movie indeed.

# PART II

# Pictures

# 17 | THE ANATOMY LESSON

Back in 2008, my neurosurgeon showed me some snaps she'd made on her cellphone of my open left forearm during a surgery she had performed on me; she offered me the pictures as evidence that her diagnosis, that I had been suffering from an entrapment of the radial nerve, had been correct. About a year later I found myself sitting in the office of another doctor, this time a neurologist. The surgery had not been effective; I had come to him for advice on whether it needed to be redone. He explained that he had good news and bad. The good news was that I didn't need another operation. The bad news was that I hadn't needed the first one either. The surgeon's diagnosis had been incorrect.

What about the pictures she had shown me? I asked.

His reply was curt. "You see what you want to see in that kind of picture."

I thought of these events as I stood before Rembrandt's 1631 painting The Anatomy Lesson of Dr. Nicolaes Tulp during a recent trip to the Netherlands. (The painting hangs in the Mauritshuis in The Hague.) *The Anatomy Lesson* shows Professor Tulp as he probes the anatomy of a cadaver's left arm with an instrument in his right hand while, with his left hand, he demonstrates the movements of which the left hand is capable and illustrates their dependence on the anatomy.

The painting is gripping in a documentary sort of way. It presents an actual event, and was painted in a lecture theater in Amsterdam that is still in use at the university. There is some dispute, I believe, about whether Rembrandt gets the anatomy of the dissected left arm of the cadaver correct. It takes knowledge to do so, of course. When it comes to cadavers, you can't just look and draw. You need to know what you see. This is true, even if it is also true, as my earlier anecdote reminds us, that false thoughts or misguided expectations can blind you to what is there (in my arm, for example, or in the photo of my arm).

Remarkably, Rembrandt seems to explore this very issue in *The Anatomy Lesson*. We begin to appreciate this when we notice the care with which he depicts the doctor's students—in particular, the way he illustrates what they are looking at, where their attention is directed. Two of them are staring straight out, at us, or perhaps at the painter himself. A third has his mind on something or someone in the audience, it appears. But four of them are engrossed in the demonstration. One seems to be looking at the teacher's face. At first I thought the other three were looking at the cadaver under investigation. But on closer inspection, their attention seems to be directed past the lifeless arm to a textbook that rests open on a stand before them. Perhaps the book performs something like the role of PowerPoint today. As Dr. Tulp lectures and dissects, he refers them to graphical representations or verbal descriptions of the relevant anatomy and physiology.

This a nice twist, and it gives the painting an epistemological weight that it would otherwise lack.

Dr. Tulp's spectators focus not on the corpse but rather on a representation, a rendition, in an illustrated book. Is this like opting for Cliffs Notes or watching the movie version?

Perhaps. Plato may have harbored the suspicion that images seduce us. According to him, we should turn away from books and pictures if we are to know things themselves.

But there is another idea—one with which Rembrandt may be experimenting—according to which there's no such thing as the direct inspection of reality; that is, there is no encounter with how things are that is not shaped or at least informed by our thoughts and pictures, and indeed by our scientific theories. From this point of view, we can think of what is on display in *The Anatomy Lesson* differently. The students are not turning away from reality when they turn their attention to the book in front of them. They are using the books and images *in order to see* what is there before them. The book teaches them to see what is there by showing them what they are supposed to see. The book gives them the knowledge necessary for comprehending vision.

In Rembrandt's painting, then, we meet a lovely epistemological circle: we need pictures (and books and theories) to assess the reality that alone provides us the means to verify and correct our pictures (and books and theories). And this goes for what Rembrandt is doing too. To make a convincing painting of the anatomy lesson, Rembrandt must be able to see it, to really see it. But as he himself shows in his picture, you need books and more pictures in order to do that.

Rembrandt's painting of a scientist at work may also be an argument for the irreducible importance of art to the scientist's basic project. There is no science without art.

# 18 | THE IMPORTANCE OF BEING DRESSED

There is a church in Florence where women and girls wearing shorts or other summer garb are made to don a blue gown upon entering. I don't know if it is an accident that the blue of the gown matches perfectly not only the painted night sky of the small cupola in the old chapel but also the field of color in the Ghirlandaio painting that hangs nearby. Far from concealing these girls and women, the effect rather is to throw them into architectural relief. Add to this the fact that the fabric, which is gauze-like and transparent, decorates and embellishes naked arms, legs, and midriffs, rather than covering them up. The whole ends up feeling like a performance or a ritual. Shades of blue float around the spacious, well-lit sanctuary, transmitting hue from place to place.

Clothes are not optional in human societies. The best guess is that the "naked ape" has been wearing clothes for thirty or forty millennia.

In her book on dress in Western painting, art historian Anne Hollander notices, as anthropologists have long known, that, when it comes to human beings, it is not nakedness that is the norm but the clothed body.[1] Nakedness is the absence of clothing, or its removal.

So it shouldn't be surprising that we make art, or ritual, or politics, out of these raw materials: who wears what where.

I don't believe that the church wardens felt anything like genuine offense or threat at the nakedness of those coming to visit the sanctuary. It's hard to find anyone in Florence in early September who is not walking around in the urban equivalent of beachwear. The threat is no more real than the determination to cover up; both are playful or pretend, but somehow urgent nonetheless.

The politics of dress, in Europe and elsewhere, is not always so benevolent. In Florence they make women cover up. But sometimes women—for example, Muslim women—are forced to uncover. *Their* insistence on covering up is a perceived threat.

I recall that when my son was three years old, back in 2006, I let him wade undressed in the waters of a lake in upstate New York. The lifeguard on duty used his megaphone from atop his perch all the way down on the other side of the beach to berate us for his nudity and threaten us with expulsion. When I was eighteen I was at Rockaway Beach in New York City with a German girl who removed her top to sunbathe. It didn't take long for the cops to arrive. As I recall, they agreed not to write her a ticket if she would cover up.

So nakedness matters and continues to matter.

My companion at the church in Florence was working herself into a rage as we waited on line to enter. Under no circumstances would she cover up! But I could tell she was disappointed that the church lady at the door was satisfied with her attire, and mine. It was only when we were inside that we realized we'd missed out on a chance to take part in this apparently universal form of social theater.

# 19 | THE ART OF THE BRAIN

A rt and science can seem so different. Scientists work in teams, in the laboratory; their progress is piecemeal, and by and large they know how to measure its occurrence. Art, in contrast, at least according to the stereotype, is personal; it is the signature achievement of the individual artist. And as for progress, well, that question doesn't really come up.

You have no doubt heard of Louis Pasteur, and of course you've heard of Charles Darwin. But have you heard of Santiago Ramón y Cajal? Along with the Italian biologist Camillo Golgi, he was awarded the Nobel Prize in Physiology or Medicine in 1906. His single and singular achievement was to produce accurate *drawings* of brain cells (neurons).

This is a remarkable example of the seminal, creative, reorienting significance of pictures in science. It is so easy to overlook the importance of *visualization* to thought and discovery. We pretend that a picture is a kind of faithful copy of what there is. But no picture is ever just that, for the simple reason that reality is too complicated. A copy of reality is just more reality. A good picture, in contrast, is the articulation of something that interests us. It is the answer to a question.

I used to have a mechanic's manual for a car that had photographs of the engine to accompany instructions on how to do maintenance. It was inferior, to me anyway, to another manual I had that consisted of line drawings of the relevant engine parts alone. The problem with the photographs was that they didn't pick out what was important. They just gave you an image of the undifferentiated stuff. The drawings, in contrast, were truly articulate; they drew your attention to what was salient even as they drew the parts themselves. They say a picture is worth a thousand words; maybe. But a drawing is worth a lot more than a mere photo. For a drawing is a thoughtful picture. It is really the visualization not just of what there is but of what matters (for a particular purpose anyway).

This is true with functional magnetic resonance imaging (fMRI) and positron emission tomography (PET) today. These technologies have revolutionized neuroscience. Not because they let us see through the skull into the brain. We know what that would look like. The brain is a lump of wet meat. No, what PET and fMRI give us is a graphical representation of what we hypothesize is going on.[1] They are more like a police sketch artist's drawing than an actual representation of the brain, for they are depictions less of the brain than of our own hypotheses.

That was no less true of Cajal's drawings. These were high-tech by the standards of the day, based as they were on the use of the microscopic examination of stained brain tissue (using a technique devised by Golgi). But more important, like the drawings in my car manual, these creations of Cajal's were realizations not so much of what Cajal merely saw—a messy arrangement under the glass—but of what he understood himself to be seeing. This is why, as the editors of a new collection of Cajal's drawings—*The Beautiful Brain: The Drawings of Santiago Ramón y Cajal*—make clear, Cajal's *drawings* supplied theoretical foundations to the emerging field of neuroscience. Cajal's drawings gave flesh to two ideas that were until then only ideas: that the unit of organization in the brain is the individual brain cell (what has come to be known as the neuron doctrine) and that cells signal each other along dendrites and axons (a theory validated only after the invention of the electron microscope, another technology of visualization). Cajal's pictures were less copies of visual information than they were renditions of a new theory of the brain. They were theoretical science.

And they were also art! I don't mean simply that they were drawings or that they were made by someone who had from his earliest years wished to pursue the life of an artist. As we learn in *The Beautiful Brain*, Cajal's physician father lured him away from a career in art by asking him to make drawings of body parts to support his own research. Eventually Cajal caught the bug and his focus shifted. No, there's something mysterious, astonishing, implausible, and imaginary about these drawings. With their captions, they are tamed. But remove the captions, or ignore them, and you are confronted with an intense and even, I want to say, intensely personal construction of line, pattern, and shape.

Some of Cajal's drawings reproduced in *The Beautiful Brain* have never been reproduced before (outside of their original publication in scientific journals). The book also contains a striking series of photographic self-portraits by Cajal himself. We have the opportunity to examine a different kind of representation, in this case of the artist/scientist as a young man, but also in middle age and finally as an old man.

# 20 | FACES AND MASKS

Portraiture fascinates because faces do, and faces matter to us because they are bound up with what it is to be a person.

I went to see Mozart's *Don Giovanni* at the Metropolitan Opera with my seven-year-old son back in 2012. It was his first opera, and he had a great time. I was struck by the fact that he found it perfectly comprehensible that Don Giovanni and his manservant Leporello could switch identities and evade their pursuers simply by exchanging their hats and cloaks. It's implausible and psychologically unrealistic to think that the Don's lovers and enemies wouldn't recognize him in the hat and cloak of his servant. Doesn't this undercut the plot? Why didn't my son think that the whole story was just silly?

In fact, there's nothing silly or implausible about this. The word *person* comes from the Latin *persona* (from the Greek *prosopon*), meaning "mask," as in the mask worn by actors on the classical stage. A person, then, in the original meaning of the term, is not the player, not the living human being, but rather the role played. By changing hat and cloak, the Don and Leporello exchanged the trappings of their different social roles and so, at least for limited purposes, they really did exchange identities.

Neither my son, nor the characters inside the drama itself, are silly because they fall for the Don's ruse; this is just the natural consequence of their taking for granted a particular way of thinking about what it is to be a person. Just as we ourselves do when we, as members of the audience, see the actor on the stage *as* the Don even though tomorrow we might see a different actor in the same role. (And just as we can tell Leporello and the Don apart on the stage even though from our seats in the back of the house we can't even really see their faces.)

Our modern conception of the person is poised awkwardly between these two poles: at one extreme the *roles we play*—Italian, aristocrat, father, lover, rogue, businessperson, et cetera—and at the other the *living human being* who appears in these roles, the one who did not choose to be born in Italy, as a man, to an aristocratic family, et cetera. We can see the tension between these different conceptions working itself out if we turn our attention to the history and development of portrait painting.

To appreciate this, consider two paintings from the permanent collection of the Städel, a museum in Frankfurt, Germany. Take first Cranach the Younger's 1550 portrait of Martin Luther. The painting gives an excellent likeness, but what it depicts is not the man, not really, but rather *his mask*, that is to say, the hat and cloak of his personality: his *face*. It might just as well have been the painting of a sculpture, for all that the man himself shows up in the piece. To give you a sense of who this person is, and that he even has a spiritual life, the painting shows him holding one of his books open to the viewer.

Now compare this with Rembrandt's 1633 portrait of Maertgen van Bilderbeecq. The face of this woman shows up here not as the mask of a person but as, in a way, the soul of a woman. This woman and her inner life are present in the picture. You can feel her heat. You can discern her thoughts and feelings. You don't need an open text to tell you who or what she is.

Three-quarters of a century separates Rembrandt's painting from Cranach's, and one might be tempted to say that Rembrandt simply knew how to depict a human face better than Cranach did. Rembrandt's paintings are more lifelike and succeed far more in making their subject matter present.

But it would be a mistake to say this, whatever your view of the relative merits of Cranach and Rembrandt. What is significant is not that they differ in their ability to capture a shared subject matter; where they differ is in their subject matter.

Cranach, painting earlier, is not painting a man; he's painting a person, that is to say, a personage. He is exhibiting a *role*—a standing and a status. The standard by which his likeness is to be assessed is not so much its match to the man as its match to our conception of the role this man played in the religious and political life of Germany. A good portrait of Martin Luther will bring him forth as a man, yes, but in something more like the way a good performance of the Don will bring forth Don Giovanni on the stage, or, to give an important example, the way in which a religious icon can succeed in bringing forth a saint.

In contrast, Rembrandt's target is not the person—not the ma-tron or wife or Dutch person or burgher—but rather the woman herself, the woman who may also be all those things but is not re-ally summed up by them. His subject matter, unlike Cranach's, is the living human being.

In the final act of the opera, Don Giovanni is dragged down to hell by an enchanted statue of a man, the Commendatore, whom the Don killed in a duel, and whose daughter the Don had seduced and cruelly mistreated. It underscores the distinction between different ways of thinking about what a person is that the Don is eventually brought to justice not at the hands of a living human being but at those of a righteous statue.

# 21 | THE PHILOSOPHICAL EYE

The painter Adolph Menzel (1815–1905) is not well known, even in his native Germany. He was tiny and ugly and he never married; he wrote in his will that "there is a lack of any kind of self-made bond between me and the outside world."[1] Perhaps this lack of bond is what made it possible for him to devote himself so totally to the task of making pictures.

Menzel drew constantly. He drew everything. He drew with his left hand and with his right. He drew on napkins and on the backs of menus. No social event was so formal or so intimate, it seems, as to quiet his active hands.

I heard a great writer say recently that her inspiration comes from an impulse to record, to document, to fix the moment, to hold on to time, to put things down.

Menzel must have shared this impulse. But there was more to Menzel's mania.

Plato thought of the painter as merely recording an image that was delivered to the senses. It's easy to make a picture of anything, he wrote; you simply hold a mirror up to it.

Anyone who has tried to draw knows that Plato got this wrong. It isn't easy to make pictures. It is painstaking. It requires physical effort and thought, and almost incomprehensible skill.

Plato's mistake went deeper. The human action of seeing is, for Plato, also akin to holding up a mirror to the world. What we see is nothing but images.

Enter Menzel, whose work embodies a commitment to the refutation of this Platonic idea.

Sure, we look about and we name what we see. But really seeing, really noticing, discerning, finding, discriminating? This is not easy and maybe not even possible.

The world is *not* a given. We need to work for it, as we need to work to build a painting or reason out a drawing. First you look here. Then you look there. The visible world outstrips what can be taken in at a glance. Seeing is active and thoughtful. It requires a philosophical eye.

And the sketches of this compulsive and unstoppable artist, no less than his oil paintings and his gouaches, are not so much documentations of what there is as investigations of the way we manufacture our own experience.

Go to the Old National Gallery in Berlin and visit with one of Menzel's smaller paintings of the 1840s, such as *The Balcony Room*. Ask yourself this question: *What do I see?* Make the time to realize how very difficult it is to say.

In my case, Menzel taught me that art can be a way of doing philosophy.

# 22 | THE CAMERA AND THE DANCE

A camera is like a big index finger directing your attention to what you are supposed to see. A movie is an edit of what is there to be seen, never a reënactment. This is why, as a general rule, film destroys dance. Dance—I don't mean dancing; I mean dance as performance—is a contact sport, an encounter of audience and performers. You can't film it, because all you can film is something that can be seen. When it comes to dance, it's not what you see but the seeing itself—the choices we make about what to pay attention to, or the way those choices are choreographed for us by the work itself—that is where the action is.

Wim Wenders's Academy Award–nominated film *Pina: Dance, Dance, Otherwise We Are Lost* contains a segment of Lutz Förster's marvelous solo from choreographer Pina Bausch's *Für die Kinder von Gestern, Heute und Morgen* (*For the Children of Yesterday, Today and Tomorrow*). I once saw this segment performed live (in the setting of Jérôme Bel's larger work *Lutz Förster*). It is a fascinating exercise in understatement and gentle, almost invisible absorption in rhythms. You watch the performer, and as you watch you shift your gaze from his hands to his hips to his breast to his leg to his enormous and beautiful nose to his not-quite-describable

73

facial expression. And he watches you with a smile, almost flirta-tiously. All this subtle play was, if not blocked from view by the large movements of the camera, then at least obscured. The subject matter switched; it was the film's own choreography that was put on display, not that of Pina Bausch.

I don't offer this as a criticism of Wenders particularly. He succeeds in offering a tribute to Bausch and giving us a glimpse of what she achieved. But it does explain the film's flatness, despite the breathtaking performances by the dancers, the unusual and pictur-esque settings, and the use of 3D. Wenders tried to film something that can't be filmed. It's like looking at your face in the mirror and trying to see the eyes you see actually seeing you. There are some things you can't see. There are some things that can't be shown.

Dance *for* film—the great work of Bob Fosse, for example, or of Fred Astaire, or the dance we see in music videos today by Beyoncé, or in Whitney Houston's early videos—is another story altogether. For these are works where the camera is itself choreographed by the dance itself, or rather, it is a collaboration, a duet, between the dancer and the camera. Dance on film, in contrast with dance for film, is usually a disappointment.

# 23 | WHY ARE 3D MOVIES SO BAD?

Technology, as a general rule, is the friend of moviemaking, as it is, I think, the friend of all the arts. Engineers design tools that afford new ways of telling stories, and film, at least the vast bulk of it, is in the business of storytelling.

The movies have always been technology-driven. This was true in the olden days. Think of what happened when sound was introduced. And it's true now. For a fascinating example, consider the case of Pixar, which started life as a hardware company; they made animations to demonstrate what could be accomplished using their products. Now they make movies (as part of Disney).

The question I want to pose is this: why are 3D movies so bad?

The problem isn't merely technical. It's not the fact that 3D darkens the screen, or the fact that 3D effects present spatial depth as visibly layered, as in a pop-up book, that accounts for what's wrong.

No, the problem with 3D is conceptual. The whole motivation for 3D movies is confused. Despite the wild success of *Avatar* and other films, 3D movies remain, I think, somewhat like pop-up books themselves; they are a childish novelty.

The question is, *why*?

The short answer is that 3D makes no contribution to cinematic storytelling. It remains at the level of the *special effect*, something like the way pop-up book technology stands in relation to the telling of the Hansel and Gretel story. 3D doesn't enable a different kind of story to be told, and critically, 3D doesn't let you see anything you couldn't see before.

The aim of the storyteller's industry is to tell you something or show you something, to exhibit a world and present you with meaningful events. Your job, as a member of the audience, is to take a look at what is given. You bring what you know and what you care about to the task of making sense of what you are shown. Both parties make a contribution. The creator gives you something to consider. You have to do the considering yourself.

Now, suppose you want an apple. I can make your craving disappear either by giving you an apple or by punching you in the stomach. In the former case, I give you what you want and I leave it to you to put the apple to its proper use (that is, to eat it). In the latter case, I eradicate your craving, but by manipulating you in a manner that has nothing really to do with apples, hunger, or desire.

3D special effects have about as much to do with storytelling as a punch in the stomach has to do with giving you what you want— that is to say, nothing.

The storyteller's job is to give you a world that is worth taking an interest in. And if you take an interest in it, you'll pay attention, and you'll think, and feel, and identify, and, yes, enjoy all manner of emotional and sensory effects. In general, art is an opportunity to explore thoughts, emotions, and sensations in just this way. But the storyteller is not in the business of *generating* the thoughts and feelings *directly*.

That's your job.

Sure, one of the things storytellers of all sorts have to do is compete for your interest and capture your attention. Bright lights, loud bangs, and, in the case of film, subtle and maybe unnoticed play with depth and focus can be put to artistic work by the storyteller. But it would be a grave mistake to take this to suggest that movies are a mere expedient for triggering events in your nervous system, or that storytelling is a kind of psychological manipulation.

I fear, however, that that's the best that can be said of 3D special effects. 3D tricks bypass story building and micromanage your sensory response. Because the value is in the story, not the response, 3D is an abdication of value.

My children and I loved *How to Train Your Dragon*, which we saw in 3D. So I don't mean to imply that application of 3D in and of itself necessarily ruins a movie.

My point rather is that when a movie in 3D is good, it's good despite the 3D and not because of it. 3D is a distraction from the story; at best it is a pleasurable *side effect*. It has nothing more to do with the film's basic content, ideas, or meaning than, say, the popcorn or the chairs in the theater do.

There is more to what is wrongheaded about our fascination with 3D movies. For one thing, conventional movies were always already in 3D! Roger Ebert makes this very point:

When you look at a 2D movie, it's already in 3D as far as your mind is concerned. When you see Lawrence of Arabia growing from a speck as he rides toward you across the desert, are you thinking, "Look how slowly he grows against the horizon"?[1]

The answer to Ebert's rhetorical question is a resounding no. We see Lawrence of Arabia move toward us along the third dimension. We don't need 3D effects to experience the three-dimensionality of depicted space.

There's a subtle conceptual issue underlying this point. In general, *representations* don't need to resemble (share properties with, look like) *what they represent*. I can describe a tomato as big, red, and spherical, and I can do so using type that is neither big nor red nor spherical. Or to use an example from the writings of philosopher Daniel Dennett: I can represent the fact that John got to the party *after* Mary by mentioning John in a sentence *before* I mention Mary.[2] Time in the representation (the sentence) needn't match time in the represented domain in order for the sentence to do a perfectly adequate job representing.

Sometimes it *is* useful to deploy a representational device that is, in relevant respects, *like* what it is used to represent. For example, to borrow an example of Wittgenstein's: Imagine that in a court of law a lawyer presents his theory of how the traffic accident occurred by setting out toy cars on a tabletop before judge and jury. In this kind of tabletop model, the actual spatial relations among the toy cars are meant to mirror and so exhibit the spatial relations among the cars allegedly involved in the accident. This is a genuinely 3D representation, and it can be an effective way of demonstrating what might or might not have happened.

As we have said already, however, it would be a big mistake to think that a representation must be 3D *in this way* to exhibit, demonstrate, or in other ways represent spatial relations.

There is a further issue lurking here: we aren't sufficiently clear about the difference between *what is represented* and mere *special effects*.

Consider again the case of our lawyer with his toy cars. The lawyer is a storyteller. He tells you what he thinks happened. He uses the toy cars to do this. The toy cars don't do the telling. They just sit there for you to consider. They show you something, but only in the context of the lawyer's presentation.

Now imagine that during his presentation the lawyer releases exhaust fumes into the room. Maybe he wants to give the members of the jury the illusion that they are in the presence of real cars with running engines. He wants to make an impact. It is worth noticing that now the lawyer is doing something entirely different from telling his story. The tabletop model displays what happened, at least according to the lawyer, and it affords the jurors the opportunity to think about what happened, or might have happened, by inspecting the construction itself. Crucially, the model does not produce in spectators the *illusion* that they are actually at the scene of the accident or in the presence of real cars! It doesn't aim at that! It aims at showing them what happened.

The fumes, however, are a special effect. In contrast with the toy cars on the table, the fumes have literally nothing to do with the accident or with what the lawyer is arguing. At best, you smell them and undergo the corresponding olfactory experience. The smell is nothing but a sideshow!

3D effects are just this kind of sideshow.

\*\*\*

Some readers of the preceding remarks, originally published on-line at the National Public Radio website, challenged my premise that 3D movies are terrible—and one even wrote to tell me that he thought I was a crotchety old relic (which I'm not).

But not everyone was negative. One person, a top executive at one of the leading 3D conversion companies in Hollywood, sent me a note expressing his complete endorsement of everything I had written.

"The bottom line," he wrote, "is those naysayers that have posted comments and accused you of being too old, or ignoring progress, are themselves cloaked in ignorance of how '3D' is not, and never will be a representation of how we see things in real life. It is in fact a gimmick, a visual sleight of hand that tends to distract from the story."

For obvious reasons, he asked me to keep his identity a secret.

The introduction of 3D technology can't be compared to that of sound, or color, or even stereo, as people like to do. And for a simple reason. We use these other technologies to show more, to extend what can be depicted. These technologies enable us to increase the amount of information we can represent or put to work in film. And this is the stuff of storytelling.

Recall Marlon Brando's famous line, as Terry Malloy, in *On the Waterfront*: "I could have been a contendah!" You recall his facial expression, posture, and movements, the line itself, the feeling with which it is delivered, but you also recall Brando's *voice*. You need sound to display the voice; you need sound for voice to be one of the elements in the composition making up the whole. Color similarly extends the working palette of the director and so extends what can be presented to an audience.

We do not similarly extend the informational content of a movie when we add 3D spatial effects. And for the simple reason that, as we noticed previously, regular film already allows us to see the spatial relations between the actors and objects that make up the scene; 3D doesn't change the palette.

Consider: Right now I can see that my coffee table is nearer to me than the dining room table. And I can see that the window is off to the right. I can also see that the window is smaller than the doorway beside it. That is, I can visually experience the three-dimensional spatial relations among the things around me.

I can also put these spatial relations in words. That's what I did in the previous paragraph. I used words to capture spatial relations such as near/far, left/right, above/below, bigger/smaller, and so on. And I can also *depict* spatial relations such as these. It is possible to make drawings, paintings, or photographs in which the spatial relations of depicted elements can be readily perceived.

None of this comes for free, by the way. Just as we need to learn the language and logic of spatial relations to describe them adequately in words, so we need to learn the methods of artificial perspective to make drawings that adequately depict spatiality. Similar issues confront the filmmaker; spatial and temporal coherence and continuity are the stuff of craft.

We get a better sense of what 3D is by comparing its introduction not to that of sound and color but rather to that of monster-sized buckets of popcorn or oversized reclining theater seats. People love popcorn and business-class seats at the movies. These greatly enhance, or at least alter, the movie-going experience. But neither has anything to do with film. And so it is with 3D. It makes a qualitative change in the movie-going experience, no doubt, but one that has about as much to do with the movie as the seat you are sitting on or the popcorn you are eating. It's a gimmick. A special effect.

And boy, there *is* an effect. No doubt about it. Just how should we describe this effect? What sort of effect is it? We've already appreciated that it has nothing to do with the representation of spatial relations. 3D does not stand to film as artificial perspective stands to painting. So what's going on?

What is sometimes claimed is that 3D gives you a greater sense of really being there, of immersion in the scene. But this is *obviously* not true. Remember, in normal life we don't usually experience the world the way we experience a 3D movie. When was the last time you ducked and exclaimed "Whoa!" when someone walked past you? When was the last time you felt a sense of dizzying motion when you looked around? If 3D were really an immersion experience, then it would be an experience of the normal, of the humdrum, of our familiar bodily location in the world where we find ourselves. But that is decidedly *not* what 3D is like. 3D is thrilling, surprising, and slightly upsetting (in a thrilling, surprising kind of way).

What 3D movies deliver is stereoscopic illusion—they manipulate where you focus and create a bizarre sense of pop-out and floating. They don't change the spatial relations you see; they change what it is like for you to experience those relations. They make them feel bizarre and they give you a thrill. For this reason, 3D is not a step in the direction of virtual reality.

Children love a feeling of bizarre pop-out and floating. Movie lovers shouldn't.

# 24 | STORYTELLING AND THE "UNCANNY VALLEY"

Many an animated character wouldn't seem so unreal and dead if it didn't seem so real and alive!

This is a puzzle that has long troubled animators. If you saw Robert Zemeckis's *The Polar Express*, you know what I'm talking about. Remember the dead eyes of the characters, their zombie-like vacancy?

Animators do an excellent job bringing the non-human to life on the screen—think of WALL-E, or the enchanted broomsticks in *Fantasia*, not to mention Mickey Mouse himself—but they falter with the more realistically human.

This precipitous drop-off in psychological reality, or in normalcy, as you get close to verisimilitude, but not close enough, was first dubbed the "uncanny valley" in 1970 by the Japanese roboticist Masahiro Mori.[1]

Lawrence Weschler describes the phenomenon and suggests the outlines of an explanation:

When a replicant's almost completely human, the slightest variance, the 1 percent that's not quite right, suddenly looms up enormously rendering the entire effect somehow creepy and monstrously alien (no longer, that is, an incredibly life-like machine but rather a human being with something inexplicably wrong).[2]

Something like this has become the standard approach. What makes animation possible in the first place, so the thinking goes, is our evolved tendency to see mind where there is none (in a sock puppet or a line drawing). This tendency runs counter to another basic cognitive trait: our natural hypersensitivity to even the subtlest inflections of face, posture, movement. The uncanny valley opens up because these two dispositions collide: we experience the mind behind the animated human-like face—just as we can project mind onto a teddy bear—but we can't help but experience it as in some way deviant, as "a human being with something inexplicably wrong."

If this gets the phenomenon right, then bridging the uncanny valley is basically a technical problem. Animators need to find ways to cover that last 1 percent by more effectively replicating the complex choreography of eyes, skin, bone, mouth, and muscle that is the genuine, animate human face. There's no obstacle in principle to bridging the valley. It's just a matter of time, money, and research collaboration between animators and cognitive scientists till they get it right.

I am not persuaded. Here's one reason why. The uncanny valley isn't confined to the moving image. A still from *Polar Express* puts the dead eye on display no less than the film itself; there are even cases of drawings that exhibit the same quality, or so I would argue. As a case in point, consider the drawings in Brian Selznick's marvelous and bizarre novel *The Invention of Hugo Cabret*.[3] The book tells the story of a homeless French boy who stumbles on one of the great pioneers of film, Georges Méliès, now employed as a toy-maker; the book delves into the impulse to make magic and to animate (bring to life) that lies at the heart of the moviemaker's art. The book is also formally experimental, using pictures not merely as illustrations, as is commonplace in books for young people, but as vehicles of narration. Whole chapters present events in drawing, and crucially, the drawings are modeled on movies. The drawings zoom in and out and seem to be governed by the logic of film editing.

The result is drawings that function according to the logic of film, rather than the logic of drawing. And the result also, or so at least I would argue, is drawings that fall into the uncanny valley. Why should this be?

The key, I think, has to do with time and narrative. Time is thick in traditional painting and illustration. Great portraits, and even not-so-great portraits, model the person or the human being, and they model them as they exist not in an instant or a time slice but rather in extended moods and situations. Portraits, in other words, are not time captures or mere stills. The latter—think of the sort of images generated by cameras mounted on street signs to catch speeders—are optical traces; they are frozen reflections. Such images are not renderings, or showings, or exhibitions. They lack rhetoric and content. And although they carry all manner of information about what they reflect, they do not really depict.

Selznick's achievement, it seems to me, is to make drawings that exist as movie stills rather than drawings, and so we read them, naturally, as devoid of the thick, forward-and-backward-in-time tension (what Husserl called protention and retention) characteristic of the lived present. Selznick's dead eye is crucially an achievement, not a defect, and it folds in on itself perfectly, harmonizing with the story's theme of film, invention, magic, and life.

How does this relate to the uncanny valley as it shows up in animated movies, which do not, after all, present themselves to us as stills of anything? My suggestion is this: we meet the uncanny valley when we disrupt the implicit rules and rhetoric that govern storytelling. Selznick violates the rules of drawing, making drawings that are more like optical stills. And animators get lost in the uncanny valley not because they fall short in regard to verisimilitude but because they lose track of the narrative rules governing their particular way of telling stories with cartoons.

Consider that writing, film, and animated film, which are (or can be) storytelling art forms, tend to be driven by and capitalize on different feelings, different stances, different kinds of desires on the part of the audience.

The basic impulse driving film as a storytelling art is the impulse to look, see, and watch; when it comes to film, we like to peep and spy. Film is the voyeuristic art. Of course we *know*, intellectually, that what we see when we watch a film is the work of directors, producers, technicians, and so on. But the thrill, the magic, the excitement of the movies comes from the feeling that we have a window onto the lives of others. Our primitive stance is that of the witness.

Fiction writing is altogether different. We may read fiction with voracious appetites, but when we do so we do not take up the stance of the voyeur, at least not typically. No, fiction is an act of *telling*, and what we encounter, or seem to encounter, when we read a novel is the storyteller. I don't mean the author or even, necessarily, the narrator. Exactly whom or what we encounter is very often in no way self-evident, and the fun may stem from working it out. It remains the case, though, that what is revealed to us, exposed, in works of fiction is not worlds that we seem to witness directly, as in the case of film, but worlds as they are presented to us by a virtual teller. Fiction is a testimonial art (and whereas film is a cult of the actor, fiction is a cult of the writer).

Now we come to animation. This occupies yet a third position. The underlying impulse behind our fascination with the cartoon is not the impulse to watch, nor is it the impulse to understand the story or the storyteller; it is, rather, the impulse *to pretend*. Cartoons put us in the mood for play, and we do not so much *watch* as we *participate*. Cartoons are the playful art.

Back to the uncanny valley. A movie like *The Polar Express* traps us in a kind of rhetorical contradiction. Insofar as the characters resemble living human beings, we are invited to take an interest in them; we feel the impulse to watch them; we are invited to take up the stance to them that would be appropriate to live-action movies. But insofar as we are watching what is manifestly an animated film, then we are at one and the same time pulled to take up the altogether opposed attitude appropriate to animation—namely, that of viewing the characters as mere playthings. We're caught in a rhetorical contradiction: real living human beings are not playthings; toys are not the sort of thing we are thrilled to watch.

Cartoons don't give us glimpses of worlds; they give us worlds to play in and toys to play with. Live-action movies, in contrast, don't give us opportunities to play; they give us access to hidden worlds. Here, then, is what I propose: the uncanny valley yawns not when animators fall short in their rendering of the human body—even if in fact they do—but rather when they get confused about what kinds of stories they are trying to tell: are they inviting audiences to pretend and play, or are they giving them an opportunity to watch? In this confusion, the story dies, and with it the light in the eyes of the characters.

# 25 | PEERING INTO REMBRANDT'S EYES

The exhibition "Late Rembrandt," which ran in 2015 at the Rijksmuseum in Amsterdam, was the first exhibition ever to focus on the adventurous and experimental painting of the last eighteen years of Rembrandt's life.

You don't need to be an art expert, let alone an expert on the works of Rembrandt, to find yourself drawn in, and puzzled, by some of these paintings (and drawings and prints). Or to find yourself looking at them with the same quizzical and interested eye with which we sometimes see Rembrandt look out at us in his self-portraits.

I was struck, walking through the galleries at the Rijksmuseum, at just how many of the figures portrayed by Rembrandt seem to have opaque and unseeing eyes. You cannot see into their oily depths; they are little black smudges. What's puzzling is that despite this fact, his figures appear lifelike and vivid—as if the viewer has an intimate access to their personalities.

How to make sense of this? Why don't we experience the figures themselves as lifeless and zombie-like, if, as it seems to me, we experience their eyes as somehow unseeing and dead?

If the eyes are "windows to the soul," then it is as if these windows are shuttered closed. But these Rembrandt paintings give the lie to this very image of eyes as windows.

As Rembrandt's near contemporary Réné Descartes argued, the soul is not present in the body the way a pilot is present in a vessel. The connection is tighter than that. And Rembrandt's pictures offer a kind of exhibition of this idea: one can encounter the manifest spirit of a living person in a picture even when there is no seeing "into" them—even, that is, when we are confined, as we are, to seeing them from the "outside."

In fact, there is no contradiction between lively spirit and lifeless eyes. Take the case of the experience of our own selves in the mirror. You can see yourself in the mirror, and you can see your eyes. But what you can't see—or, rather, what you can't really experience—is the fact that it is *these very eyes that you now see* that are doing the seeing. Instead, what you encounter when you try to look into your own eyes in a mirror are mere objects, sightless, foreign, blank.

Maybe this is the key to what goes on in Rembrandt's portraits. He presents his personalities to us as we would encounter ourselves in the mirror: intimately, immediately, and with understanding, but from the outside.

Now, there is a group of portraits by Rembrandt that are in an entirely different key—his self-portraits. In these paintings, almost miraculously, there is no question of lifeless or unseeing eyes. With the self-portraits the subject is *not* presented to us as we see ourselves in the mirror (even though these pictures, self-portraits, are actually made using mirrors!). In observing these paintings, we don't so much look at Rembrandt as we encounter him looking back at us. He is active and inquiring. And so he is alive in a way that the other portrayed figures are not. We encounter him as a person rather than, so to speak, as an object.

The differences I have described between the blank eyes we see in almost every figure painting by Rembrandt in this exhibition and the animate gaze of the self-portraits is not so much a difference in what the viewer actually sees—that is, it's not a literal difference in what is visible—but a difference in the *acts* these paintings perform.

These works show different kinds of things and invite us to take up different kinds of relations to what they show.

# 26 | THIS IS NO ZOO

The Civic Museum of Natural History in Milan contains a magnificent collection of dioramas. The museum was badly damaged during the Second World War, so the oldest of them dates back no further than the 1950s. But the diorama form is very much alive and well in this museum, as indeed in some other natural history museums around the world. There are more than a hundred dioramas in the Milan collection, and at the time of my visit they were about to add three brand-new ones.

Which is somehow surprising. Diorama seems so old-fashioned. It dates back to the era before widespread access to color photography, not to mention to a time when free digital access to information and graphical media would have been considered science fiction. Indeed, everything you see in a diorama is a collaboration of science and craft or science and art. Every leaf, for example, in the diorama jungle will have been hand-cut and hand-painted. And even the animals, which are usually genuine, have been subject to the taxidermist's handiwork.

There is also the fact that the animals in a diorama are stiff. And not only because they are stuffed. They are stiff also because there is something theatrical about the way they are staged or posed.

This, in turn, I think, has everything to do with the fact that there is a pane of glass separating us and them.

Ask yourself: why the glass? This is no zoo and there's no danger of anything breaking out. Nor is there any reason to think that people are going to invade diorama exhibits. No, the glass has a different sort of function. It provides a frame. It works like the curtains bunched in a cord at either end of a theatrical stage. It is the pane separating us from the world of the diorama. Without the glass, you're just looking at stuff in front of you. With the glass, you are peering, as if by magic, into a world remote in space and time.

But here's the rub. You need the pane of glass to enable the illusion. But so long as there is, obviously, a pane of glass between you and the diorama, there won't be much of an illusion at all. You don't occupy a God's-eye view on a polar bear or a snow leopard or an African elephant. You're in Milan, after all, and the model animal is in the same room as you.

This reminds us that illusion may not be quite the right category for the experience of a diorama. We are, rather, in the domain of make-believe. When we look at a diorama, we only pretend to see what it shows us.

In Milan there is one diorama where a tree casts shadows *on the sky* (that is, the physical model of the tree casts shadows on the ceiling, which was painted blue to look like the sky). Very few of the people in my tour group noticed this. I didn't. It had to be called to my attention. I think this is not because we didn't notice the sky, or because the painted backdrop created a perfect sky illusion. It's because we were only pretending it was the sky anyway.

I mention this because it may be that the quaintness and old-world quality of dioramas have something to do with the way they invite pretend—and, with it, play—to happen. And this may also explain the remarkable fact that, despite their quaintness, diorama thrives as an exhibition mode in today's high-tech culture.

My tour guide in Milan bemoaned the fact that the public tends to think of not just diorama but natural history museums in general as kids' play, not stuff for serious grown-ups. Not so, he insisted. Natural history museums are places for research and knowledge creation and art/science collaboration.

He may be right about that. But natural history museums are also places for magic, pretend, and play, as we have just been considering. Maybe grown-ups don't do that so well. In fact, maybe we can't do it the way we used to do it as children. You can organize all the evening cocktail parties you like at the museum, to draw in the adult crowd, but that won't get the grown-ups to use the pane-of-glass portal the way children know how to do.

# PART III

# Art's Nature

# 27 | COUGHING AND THE MEANING OF ART

In 2010 I attended a Keith Jarrett solo piano recital at Davies Symphony Hall in San Francisco. The hall, which seats nearly three thousand people, was sold out.

The first time an audience member coughed, Jarrett stopped playing and commented on the excellent timing of the cough. As others coughed, he pretended to express concern about possible contagion, wondering aloud, somewhat bitterly, why it was that people always got colds at his shows, and noting how surprising it is that he never gets colds at his own shows. Before long he was berating the audience, admonishing them to shut up, and comparing this San Francisco crowd to anti-American audiences in Europe in the 1970s.

The audience was enraged. "Just play, will you!" men shouted. People stormed out in droves.

This was not the first time I saw an artist freak out onstage about coughing in the audience. Back in the 1990s I attended an evening with the performance artist Karen Finley at the American Repertory Theater in Cambridge, Massachusetts. The hall was packed.

As I recall, Finley was enacting her experience of her brother's death by AIDS. She addressed the dead brother as though he lay there dying and she was at his bedside.

A member of the audience coughed uncontrollably. The coughing wouldn't stop.

Finally, visibly enraged, Finley walked to the footlights, peered out into the gloom, and angrily demanded that the offending individual leave.

I remember that the audience felt ashamed for her. As a friend of mine remarked at the time, for all *she* knew, the person in the audience coughing was sick. Maybe he had AIDS.

Which brings me to today's theme. Most people attending live performances are not sick. But then why is there so much coughing at live performances?

I've seen articles in theater programs suggesting that the cause is bad posture and urging audience members to readjust their posture if they feel a fit of coughing coming on.

But this can't be the right explanation. Nobody coughs at the movies, and most people slouch at the movies.

I learned recently that the director of one large musical forum is convinced that the problem has to do with humidity levels. By raising humidity levels, he believes, he can eliminate the epidemic of coughing that breaks out each night during shows.

I find this entirely implausible. After all, if the coughing were brought on by an environmental condition of this sort, wouldn't the musicians cough too? And as Keith Jarrett bemoaned onstage that night in San Francisco, *he* never coughs at his own concerts.

Actually, Jarrett's remark points us in an interesting direction. Jarrett doesn't cough when he's playing because he's busy. He has something to do. His attention is absorbed (more or less!) in the task at hand. Not so the audience. When you are a member of a live audience, it's your job to sit there, be still and silent, and *pay attention*.

Paying attention isn't easy. It requires knowledge—just what are you supposed to be paying attention to? And it requires skill. In my view, one of the sources of art's value is that it gives us an opportunity to pay attention and perceive what after all may require quite an effort to make sense of or appreciate. Art is an opportunity to cultivate in ourselves the ability to comprehend and perceive what is going on.

Jarrett's and Finley's outbursts remind us that even the performers have trouble staying focused. This brings out what is all too obvious: namely, that the audience too is performing, and that the audience too is on display.

Surely that's the big difference with the movies. You are *not* on display as you sit in the dark at the cinematic spectacle. You are gone. You are invisible. You are transported.

It's never that way at a live performance. And that's precisely because the performers are in the room too, with you, and, as we have been considering, they are aware of you and responding to you.

So why do people cough at live performances? Well, one answer is clear. They are uncomfortable. They are uncertain. They are, very often, bored out of their minds. And they are under pressure *not* to cough.

That's a recipe for bringing out the scratchy throats if anything is. This also explains why paying attention to your posture might help you stop coughing even if bad posture isn't the cause of the coughing in the first place. It gives you something to do, after all.

So one way to get the audience to stop coughing would be to make the performance more movie-like—louder, brighter, bigger. Or more like a sporting event. The soccer great Zinedine Zidane has said that when he plays before a crowd of eighty thousand people, he doesn't even know they are there. He is *in his game*.

But performance is not like the movies or a sporting event. The point can never be to pretend that the audience is not there.

So the only alternative is to embrace the audience, and embrace their need to make noise and be heard. For that's what's really going on. Audiences cough to remind you that they are there and to let you know that they are uncomfortable. Artists and audiences both need to acknowledge that this discomfort is not a bad thing. In fact, it's what the audience is paying for.

Upshot: coughing at shows is *not* a problem.

Back to my evening with Keith Jarrett in San Francisco. Once the audience had thinned out, we were left alone with a piano player who had now put fully on display just how fragile his own powers of concentration were, just how delicate his own ability to make the event happen was. At one point, he laid his head down on the keys and explained almost tearfully that the coughing had made him settle for an ending that disappointed him.

And then something remarkable happened. Everything changed. The audience's anger at the self-indulgent performer transformed itself into a sense of love for the artist who was, after all, right there on the stage before us all, trying to make himself into someone who could make it happen. He was struggling.

Jarrett went on to play for hours. There were five encores. And no one noticed if people were still coughing.

# 28 | IS IT OKAY IF ART IS BORING?

Do you remember being bored as a kid? I do.

I remember long stretches of unstructured time with nothing to do. Time reduced to a kind of metronome, second after second, or sensation after sensation. I remember being confronted by the irritating sense that I was trapped, caught, in unending time.

Boredom comes in different shapes and sizes. But I find that adults do not very often encounter this distinct, metronomic type of boredom.

We don't live by the metronome as grown-ups. We live, rather, by *the project*. A dinner may take a few hours; the writing of a book or the raising of a child may take many years. But these are the sorts of organized activities that span arcs, with beginnings, middles, and ends, that structure our lives and shoot us into a curve that soars above the axis of linear time.

It is a commonplace that time seems to accelerate as you get older. I suspect this has to do with the tendency of these projects—and organized arcs of significance—to control our whole lives more and more the older we get.

But there is one place in my adult life where I have known the same boredom that I associate with childhood: it is in the vicinity of art. I think of what it is like to be stuck in a middle seat during a long performance, or that sinking feeling that comes over me when, after the lines and the coat check, I now find myself confronted with *another* gallery, a room full of more pictures hanging impassively and inactively on the walls.

At one performance I attended with a friend, he remarked on how "dull" the experience was. What's curious, what demands attention, is this: I don't think my friend meant that the show we'd sat through was no good. It was boring, yes, but not necessarily bad just because it was boring.

Works of art, in all their variety, it seems to me, *afford* us the opportunity for boredom—and they do so when everything in our lives mitigates against boredom. Maybe this is one of art's gifts? Could it be that the power to bore us to tears is a clue to what art is and why it is so important?

Some artists, we know, aim at boredom. The composer John Cage comes to mind. But I'm drawn to the more radical possibility that *all* art points toward boredom, not exactly as its goal, but as its foreseeable consequence. Or as one of its mechanisms.

Why should this be?

Art induces, in a sense, a temporary illiteracy or, even more, a temporary blindness. Works of art say: "I may be a portrait, or a still life, but unlike the photograph in this morning's newspaper, or the snapshot in your wedding album, there is no caption that you can think up—nor is there one written on the wall, even if there is one written on the wall—that settles, once and for all, what I am doing, what I am showing, whether I am showing anything at all, and if I am, why I am doing it."

Art in this sense interrupts the arc—or disturbs. It unveils us to ourselves. It forces us to recognize all that we take for granted that ordinarily makes it possible to know, without even thinking about it, what something is or what is happening. Art precludes, maybe only momentarily, the skillful fluency that ensures intelligibility. And surely one natural response—not the only response, to be sure, but one that is always there in the offing as a possible response—is boredom.

This is the same kind of boredom that you might encounter in works of philosophy. You can't dip into philosophy for an answer to this or that. This is because philosophy, unlike physics, doesn't produce nuggets of truth or fact. In philosophy there is no bottom line—there is no answer that can be placed in the archives.

Art and philosophy are in this way alike. If we measure them according to familiar standards of utility, or practical value, or application, well, then, they may fall short. And insofar as we are caught up in those standards and expectations, well, then, art and philosophy are liable to bore us, for they interrupt what we are doing and they demand that we break not just with what keeps boredom at bay but with so much of what we take for granted that makes ordinary organized living possible.

Art's boredom, like philosophy's, is a valuable boredom. This boredom itself is an aspect of art's *work*, its power to disrupt and, in disrupting, reveal us to ourselves.

I said the work of art challenges you to perceive it or bring it into focus. The work of art, as I put in my book *Strange Tools*, says: "See me, if you can! I dare you!"

But works of art don't just present themselves as obscure and out of focus. They also, I think, are required—by what the choreographer Jonathan Burrows has referred to as a kind of implicit contract—to give you the resources that you require to make sense of them. Works of art, then, are contractually guaranteed opportunities to move from not seeing to seeing, or from not getting it to getting it.

Boredom can be a symptom of the fact that we are out of our comfort zone.

When it comes to art, and philosophy, there isn't even anything that rises to the level of an encounter until you experience the fact that it is not the work—not the picture, or play, or dance, or song, or installation—that is opening itself up, but you yourself, and all of us together.

# 29 | THE OPPORTUNITY OF BOREDOM

D r. Taub, one of the characters in the old television show *House*, has infant twins. He loves them and wants to care for them. The problem is that he finds spending time with them unbearably boring.

Their books put him to sleep. He finds it awkward and unnatural to engage in their play. Taub feels inadequate as a father. I have felt the same way at times.

It's great to be with your kids, especially while you do something else. (My infant daughter sleeps beside me as I type this.) Judging by all the mothers paying more attention to their smartphones than their children while sitting on park benches, this is probably not an unusual phenomenon.

I went to a screening of Andrei Tarkovsky's film *Stalker* at the New School in Manhattan in 2012. There was a panel discussion, and Geoff Dyer, who had a new book out about *Stalker*, warned those in the audience who hadn't seen the film that they ran the risk of getting bored. The movie was very slow, he explained; *very* little happened. He ventured that they'd suffer less if they knew right at the outset that this film was no *Bourne Identity*. It has a totally different kind of pacing. We could eliminate boredom, or at least mitigate it, Dyer seemed to suggest, by adjusting our expectations at the outset.

So, what is boredom, anyway?

It is a state of discomfort, to be sure. It's a state in which we find ourselves uninterested, perhaps because we are disinterested and detached.

One might say that boredom is the besetting sin of art—in all its varieties: performance, painting, sculpture, film, writing, et cetera—but also of the lecture hall and the classroom. My ten-year-old son is bored in school. What more withering criticism of his teachers could one find? And indeed, describing a movie or book or theatrical performance as boring is about as damning as it gets.

If you stop to think about it, though, the link between art and formal education, on the one hand, and boredom, on the other, may be, if not exactly unavoidable, then to a certain degree inevitable.

Consider that what all of these—performance, writing, teaching, and so on—have in common is the structure of detachment. Pupils sit and listen to a teacher. Audiences pay to watch and scrutinize, but they must keep quiet and sit in the dark. Visitors to the gallery can look and think but not touch. These events are structured by detachment. That's where they begin, on the verge of boredom. Boredom is the baseline from which they can, at most, strive to deviate.

Some artists, writers, and teachers see boredom as the enemy; they battle it the way firefighters battle a blaze. In their effort to deviate from the baseline, from boredom, they *engage* the audience. They try to pull down the wall separating them from the kids, or the audience, or the visiting public. At its best, they do this by, in effect, putting on display a thing of value—knowledge, a story, a sculpture, a painting, whatever—while also providing the tools the audience needs to understand it. For instance, a piece of music may begin by introducing a theme, thus giving the audience the resources to know what to pay attention to as the theme is developed in the sequel.

This strategy also runs some pretty high risks. At the end of the day, the sort of engagement provided by art is only ersatz. You don't really know or really care about Romeo and Juliet, or the Stalker and his clients, or Jason Bourne.

Indeed, at its worst, the impulse to deny boredom finds its expression in mere stagecraft and manipulation, in the willingness to pander and entertain. We find this tendency at work even in education, where teachers are increasingly pressured to think of their students as, in effect, customers who need to be kept happy so they keep coming back for more.

There is another approach to boredom in the arts, one that is perhaps more common in the avant-garde. If boredom stems from detachment, and if some measure of detachment is unavoidable in art (and in life), then getting bored is not just an irritating state, it's an opportunity.

This seems to be how Tarkovsky thought about *Stalker*. When the studio supporting the film asked him to think more of the audience and pick up the pace, he responded by slowing things down even more. He was trying to be boring.

Or take the case of John Cage. I understand he was invited to give an important series of lectures at Harvard toward the end of his life. As I heard the story, he produced his three lectures by randomly mixing words from three books of note—one of them was Wittgenstein's *Tractatus*, I believe—and he then simply read the word salad aloud. Eventually his audience had dwindled to two or three people. He'd been very, very boring. But by affording his listeners maximal detachment—there were no ideas to get, no plot to follow, no meaning to perceive—he had afforded them a different kind of freedom, to think, to let the mind wander, or to contemplate what was happening.

Detachment may be unavoidable in the arts. It is not unavoidable in life (even if conflicts about our attachments may be).

I think Dr. Taub ended up getting it just right. He realized that he can spend time with his kids not by watching them or trying to be one of them but by doing his own thing with them. So he read the girls articles about the NFL. His enthusiasm was contagious. They couldn't understand anyway. They all had a good time. Taub stopped being bored by his kids when he stopped looking, perceiving, watching, and thinking and figured out how to just hang out with them.

# 30 | ART PLACEBO

I don't know whether it is true that a janitor at an art gallery was fired for sweeping up the artwork the morning after the opening. But the story captures a certain skepticism about art: if art is whatever "we," or the art cognoscenti, say it is, then there is no such thing as art.

The worry that art is a sham is an old idea, and it is one that art itself has cherished. The confounding of folk ideas about what art is and what it is not is one of twentieth-century art's most flamboyant gestures and familiar clichés.

But skepticism about art takes more subtle and more interesting forms.

Psychology and neuroscience give rise to suspicion from a different angle. From the point of view of these fields, works of art trigger experience, and experience is a neurological effect. This means that the art itself doesn't matter, not really. Art produces aesthetic experiences the way pills affect the body's chemistry. And anyway, most psychologists are content to identify the aesthetic experience with the fact of your liking something. Since what we like is not confined to art, the implication is clear, even if it is not usually noticed: we can't draw a meaningful line between what is and what is not art.

Skepticism isn't confined to outsiders. This is one way to read Michael Fried's famous 1967 rejection of Tony Smith's sculpture and other work Fried characterized as theatrical or literal.[1] For Fried, as I read him, such works aren't really art at all. They're masquerade art. There is no art in mere place or scale or expanse, and it is never art merely to stage an encounter with these. Real art is meaningful articulation; it is not found but made, the result of human decision-making. Minimalist sculpture of the sort Fried takes Smith's work to exemplify occludes genuine art-making; it gets in the way of our doing the work we need to do as viewers to understand art.

Fried's view is not exactly skeptical. After all, he starts from the idea that artists and art culture have turned their back on art. Fried says no to what he calls minimalism because, for him, minimalism says no to art. But I think we can see a kind of skeptical impulse at work nonetheless, for at bottom what Fried articulates is the thought that what passes for art among us is not really art at all. (Perhaps one can say: Fried criticizes theatrical art because it conforms to neuroscience's wrongheaded psychological-trigger theory. For what is a minimalist work other than an experience trigger? That's what makes it theatrical.)

The worry that there might be art imposters on the prowl is certainly a live one in today's environment—or rather, market, where prices are high and where there are, by now, too many examples of experts being taken in by frauds.

Reflecting on this state of affairs, the critic Blake Gopnik observes that every time a connoisseur is fooled by a fake, the forger has taught us that connoisseurship is not to be trusted.[2] Gopnik is attacking the myth of the connoisseur, the idea that some people, the experts, can tell just by looking whether a work is an original, and so whether it is a thing of value, whether it deserves the value we assign it. He also insists, provocatively, that where a forgery does fool the knowledgeable eye of the expert, we have no reason whatsoever not to think of the fake as on a par with the original. It's the artist's idea that matters, not the causal involvement of his or her hands, and if the forgery fools us, interests us, gives us pleasure, this can only be because it makes a move, does something, in the very space of the artist's ideas. For Gopnik, it is really prejudice to think that one work is better than another because of who made it. If the works are not discriminable at the level of what even the connoisseur can see, then the works are not different in value. Not really.

Like Fried, Gopnik is affirming a conception of art that resists falling in line with current dogma or practice. For Gopnik there is something misguided about the whole business of connoisseurs and attribution. As he writes, what it is to be a Rembrandt is just not the same as what it is to be by Rembrandt's hand.

Notice that Gopnik strikes a familiar skeptical pose—that of the person on the street—when he insists that it is a myth that there are art world insiders (connoisseurs, critics) with special powers of sensitivity. But I also detect an unacknowledged psychologism at work in Gopnik's position, and so a more thorough-going skepticism about art. This comes out in the idea that forgery is valuable because it yields pleasure; that the non-expert's pleasure is no less authoritative than that of the critic, and that the pleasure of the fake is no less authentic than that of the original; in the suggestion that if two works, or two objects, are identical in respect to their subjective effects—if they yield the same quotient of pleasure—then they must be the same in respect to value; that differences in provenance can only be of indirect (e.g., historical) interest.

It is right to reject, as Gopnik does, the myth of the connoisseur. But he may do so for the wrong reasons. The problem with the myth, really, is not that it attributes unrealistic powers of discernment and identification to the connoisseur or critic, but rather that it mischaracterizes the expert's job, and so it misunderstands what powers that person needs to do the job well in the first place.

Gopnik describes the connoisseur as if he or she were a human measuring device, someone who has been trained to give the right answer to questions of value and origin. This thought leads directly to the kind of skepticism I am trying to bring into view. For either we suppose that the connoisseur cannot be wrong, that whatever he or she says goes, or we suppose that mistake is possible. But if we choose the latter, it seems, we must admit that there are no settled criteria for deciding whether a work of art is of genuine value; there is only what you or I or we "like."

The connoisseur/critic, crucially, is not a measuring instrument, a kind of authorship- or value-detector. Critics, rather, are bent on seeing, and seeing is not mere detection. Unlike detecting, seeing is not instantaneous, nor is it all or nothing, or once and for all. We might say that seeing itself is thoroughly critical; it is thoughtful and it is contextual. Stanley Cavell, the philosopher, captures this idea: what distinguishes the critic is not that he or she can discern qualities that you cannot, but rather that, in discerning them, the critic can give you the means to discern them as well. Criticism is less an art of discrimination than it is a discipline of accounting for what one sees; it is a practice of making it intelligible to oneself and another.[3] Critics make sense, and they give you the tools you need to make sense too. Critics don't just see; they teach us how to see.

It is a commonplace—stressed by *New Yorker* art critic Peter Schjeldahl, commenting on Gopnik—that fakes expose themselves in time.[4] They are designed to fool their audience; new audiences that come along later aren't likely to be taken in. Schjeldahl concludes that the pleasures—he uses Gopnik's word—provided by the fake are false pleasures that will soon reveal themselves for what they are.

I want to agree with Gopnik that engagement with a fake can yield not only genuine pleasure but also insight into an artist's work. But this is not because it fools, or will eventually fail to fool the expert. That's a red herring. It turns out that nothing that we might be wrong about is relevant, in the final analysis, to what we make of what is there before us. But that is where the important pleasures of art are to be found, not in first impressions or brute reactions, to be sure, nor from mere registrations or detections, but rather in active, critical engagement with what there is. From this point of view, the skeptical anxiety that we might be wrong and not know it has no force.

But this can't be right! Surely it is possible to be wrong, flatly, objectively, factually, about whether an object is by Vermeer, say, or Rembrandt? Here I think Gopnik is exactly right. The point is not so much that the question of value and that of authorship come apart. The point is that the question of authorship isn't the same as the question of whether the artist's hands were involved in the making. Once you recognize the possibility that a painting could be a Titian even though it is primarily the work of his studio assistants, then you can allow that a painting can be a Vermeer even though it is a forgery. As Gopnik thinks of it, you can think of the forger as a studio assistant who came upon the scene after the artist was gone, making a picture that the artist himself never got around to making.

Yes, critics can be wrong. But their mistakes are not misfirings, as if they said yea when they should have said nay. Critics go wrong when they misunderstand the significance, the importance, of what they see.

What is striking to me, then, is that, far from diminishing the connoisseur/critic, this line of thought helps us appreciate what he or she really does. It is the work of the connoisseur/critic— whether professional or amateur—to discern what a work is doing and so what work it is.

John Dewey writes: "By one of the ironic perversities that often attend the course of affairs, the existence of art objects upon which the formation of an esthetic theory depends has become an obstruction to theory about them."[5]

The artwork is not the object, says Dewey; the artwork is the experience the object affords. Crucially, Dewey rejects the idea that experiences are interior, private, sensation-like occurrences triggered by events out there in the external world. That is, he rejects the way of thinking about sensory events that neuroscience tends to take for granted. For Dewey, as I understand him, experiences are *made*; they are transactions with the world around us; they are, in fact, exercises of a kind of criticism or critical seeing (to use a phrase of Meyer Schapiro's).[6]

If we follow Dewey in rejecting a psychologized conception of experience, this opens up the possibility of taking seriously a new, more positive, non-mythological conception of the connoisseur or the critic.

We are all critics, and neither the possibility of forgery nor that of perceptual error should lead us to be skeptics, about art or anything else.

# 31 | ARE WORKS OF ART RELICS?

In an essay published in the *Brooklyn Rail* in 2014, New York University art historian Alexander Nagel argues that it's time to move beyond the relic or cult model of artworks that, he believes, has shaped our attitudes to art since about 1700.[1]

Members of a religious cult cherish and venerate a tunic not because there's anything special about the ratty old garment but because, so they believe, the garment was once worn (let's say) by a saint. Whether something is a relic, therefore, is not the sort of thing you can see, just as you can't see by looking at a person that he or she woke up in New York City this morning. Of course, there may very well be visible clues about a would-be relic's origins. Following up on these and authenticating the relic is a job for the historian, or the scientist, or perhaps the detective.

And so, according to Nagel, we have come to think of works of art as valuable not for their intrinsic, manifest features but rather because of who made them, or when, or under what conditions. A Pollock painting may be worth millions, but a copy, one that was not made by his hand, even one that fools the experts, is worth nothing. Commenting on a recent Abstract Expressionism forgery scandal, Nagel suggests that Abstract Expressionism may be particularly vulnerable to copying. Not because the paintings in question are easier to copy than paintings in other styles, but rather because the Abstract Expressionists, at least by the lights of their champions, so rigorously adhere to the relic conception. They are invested in the idea that the works were the unmediated, direct, pure expression of the creative hand of the artist.

The idea that our attitudes to art are shaped by a relic model makes sense of the fact that we value originals more than copies; it makes sense of the way we think of connoisseurs, according to which they are, essentially, detectives whose job it is to pursue the traces left on a canvas back to its historical origin. And finally, the relic/cult model explains why we, as a culture, are so anxious about art forgery.

It was not always so, explains Nagel. In the Renaissance, for example, before the supposed advent of the relic model, it was widely supposed that excellent copies inherited the quality of their originals. In this setting, copying was not a crime and forgery not really even possible. Nagel tells how one collector, when asked by a friend for a painting in her possession, responds that she will give it gladly once she's had a chance to get a copy made for herself. And religious icons are, precisely, copies whose manner of reproduction licenses putting them to use in the service of religious practice. An appropriately reproduced icon is an icon, just as an appropriately copied chess set is a chess set.

Nagel is on to something. But I wonder if he's right that we are in the grip of the relic/cult conception. Could our attitudes to art be quite that irrational? And anyway, it seems to me that there is much in our attitudes to artworks that doesn't fit with the relic conception. Sure, we care who made a work, when, and under what conditions, but when we care about art we also care about the works themselves, their look and their meaning. We engage with the paintings: we study them, we think about and interrogate the works themselves. None of that makes sense on the relic conception.

By the same token, I reject the idea that connoisseurs are measuring instruments for determining what a work is by tracing it back to its historical origin. Not that they do not sometimes do just that: identifying the value of a thing by discerning where it comes from. But it is not the *origins* that make the thing valuable; it is, rather, that origins—who made something, when, and why—bear on what sort of value the works themselves might have. Connoisseurs look, evaluate, and seek to find the words to describe what they see and why they judge as they do, and so they aim to persuade others to see things as they do. They are educators, not detectors.

In place of the relic model, I offer what you might call the conversation model. According to the conversation model, works of art are gestures, or utterances, or moves in an ongoing dialog or conversation. The value of a work consists, then, in the originality of its contribution to this ongoing exchange, or perhaps just in the wit with which it takes up the play of ideas. The work is valuable, on this view, because it is a datable foray into an ongoing and historically changing conversation.

The conversation model lets us make sense of the advent of forgery. On the conversation model, passing off a copied work of art as an original is like passing off a fake bank check. A bank check is authentic only if it bears a valid signature, but not because we think of checks on the relic model. Rather, only if the check was signed in the right way by the right person is it a commitment to make payment. And so with works of art: regardless of what the painting appears to say or mean, it fails to say or mean anything if, in fact, no one ever really put it forward, in the right time and place, as a proposition.

And that's true even if there is no way to tell by inspecting the object itself whether it is in fact "an original." From the standpoint of the conversation model, a copy is worth less than an original even if we can't tell the two apart. Authenticity transcends verification, not because we think of artworks as relics (just as we don't think of checks as relics) but rather because our relations to others—our place in the ongoing conversation—are themselves always inevitably a problem for us; that problem is just not something we can ever hope to eliminate by mere inspection of the material conditions.

# 32 | REPRODUCTIONS IN THE AGE OF ORIGINALITY

The first time I laid eyes on Michelangelo's *Pietà* (1497–1500) in St. Peter's Basilica at the Vatican, I let out a sob. I honestly don't know why. I was surrounded by a dense crowd of tourists; the sculpture was set back behind a thick plexiglas panel. Whatever view I was able to enjoy was punctuated by the lights of autofocus cameras reflected in the intervening barrier. Despite the noise and distraction, or maybe because of it, I found myself moved by the figure—the frail, boyish body of the dead Jesus limp across the lap of his powerful (indeed, disproportionately large) grief-stricken mother.

I didn't have that sort of emotional reaction when I got to see the *Pietà* again in London, when it was on display as part of the exhibition "Michelangelo and Sebastiano" at the National Gallery in 2017. This time I was able to get right up to the object and examine it in all its striking detail for as long as I wanted, undisturbed by the throngs I had encountered at St. Peter's.

I was not surprised to discover that the *Pietà* on display in London was not Michelangelo's original, but rather an exact replica manufactured in 1975. Might this fact, that it was a *copy*, explain my different response?

It turns out that this was not the only copy among the works gathered together at the National Gallery for this show. There is a Giulio Clovio copy of a study for a painting by Michelangelo that is now lost. And there is a late nineteenth-century cast of Michelangelo's *The Risen Christ* (1519–1521), the original of which is to be found in Santa Maria sopra Minerva, in Rome. (There is also an earlier, defective version of the same theme on display, this one finished by an unknown artist sometime in the seventeenth century.)

Indeed, the show's high point is a remarkable new reproduction of the Borgherini Chapel in the church of San Pietro in Montorio, in Rome. The wall text does little to emphasize the remarkable imitation of the chapel that is on display: "This masterpiece [the chapel itself] is reproduced here at slightly reduced scale, using digital recording and printing technology." You need to go to the website of Adam Lowe's Factum Arte group in Madrid to get a sense of what an extraordinary technological and artistic achievement this is. The Factum Arte team documented, digitally recorded, and then rebuilt the whole chapel, using a combination of contemporary materials and technologies as well as old styles of plasterwork and construction. What results is a reproduction not of the original chapel as it was intended but of the original as it survives today in Rome. Everything from chipped paint and pockmarked plaster to the existence of a twentieth-century Italian wall outlet embedded in the Renaissance plasterwork is recreated.

The result is breathtaking. I overheard the woman standing next to me in the museum exclaim: "It's incredible. I feel like I've been transported to Italy."

Now, there is something vaguely Westworld-like or Disney-like about this kind of pretend. But in an era such as our own, when most of us learn about the world's great works of art from reproductions in books or even lower-quality pictures on the internet, it's hard to deny the immense cultural value of this sort of convincing reproduction. I haven't seen the original chapel in Rome, but I can describe it to you.

I actually visited the original of *The Risen Christ*. The original in the Roman church, I recall, is partially covered, presumably out of consideration for Christ's physical modesty, or our own. It is only in the copy that I was afforded an unobstructed view, as it were, of the original.

But there are other, subtler reasons why this show's reliance on copies and reproductions is strikingly appropriate.

Nowadays, as the New York University art historian Alexander Nagel has argued, we as a culture tend to adhere to something like a relic conception of the work of art. We value the painting not just for what it is in itself but, rather like a relic, for its presumed provenance. We, as a culture, participate in the cult of the originally produced work. For this reason, a mere copy, however informative as to the quality of its original, can never be a thing of commensurable value in its own right.

But it was not always so. In the "copy cultures" of the past, works of art lived in and through their copies. Nagel gives many examples. In ancient Rome, copies of Greek statues were viewed as legitimate substitutes for their originals. And the tradition of the Byzantine icon was based on the idea that an icon was an adequate image of God or a saint just insofar as it was an adequate copy of another sound icon. Nagel recounts that when Renaissance art collector Isabella d'Este "is asked by an aristocratic friend for her painting of Mary Magdalene, she replies that she would be happy to send it, but only asks for time to have a good copy made."[1]

The transition from a copy culture to a cult of original production is one that seems to have taken place in Michelangelo's day. Indeed, as a young man, Michelangelo endeavored not only to imitate his elders but also to make something more like forgeries of their works, even going so far as to age and "distress" these to make them appear older than they really were.

So it is somehow fitting that the curators of this exhibition have made free use of copies. In doing so, and in doing so with such a light touch, they cast illumination on the fact that in the age of Michelangelo and Sebastiano, the status of a copy would have been uncertain and problematic.

(I bought an exhibition postcard with a detail of the *Pietà*. Although it was a postcard for *this* exhibition, I was surprised to discover it shows a picture of the original St. Peter's *Pietà*. It's as if the copy in the show functions solely as a stand-in for the original and has no relevant qualities of its own. A documentation of the show needn't concern itself with the copy. For all intents and purposes, it's as if the original *was* transported to London. Or maybe the point goes the other way around: for the purposes of documenting the fake in London, a photo of the original is just as good.)

Actually, there's an even more interesting way in which this show engages with the problem of relics and copies. At the heart of the relic conception of the artwork is the idea that artworks carry powers bestowed on them by their authors or creators. Great artworks flow from the creative powers of great artists. And what makes an artwork special is that it can be traced directly to its creative source.

But it is just this picture of the artist as a solitary font of creativity that is called into question by this show with its focus on Michelangelo and Sebastiano's remarkable twenty-five-year-long friendship and, crucially, their collaboration.

Typically exhibitions built on the pairing of artists start from the curator's thought that one artist's work sheds light on the other's. This is the case, for example, with the Matisse/Diebenkorn show at the San Francisco Museum of Modern Art, or with the Rubens and Rembrandt show up in 2017 at the National Gallery in London.

But the situation is altogether different when it comes to "Michelangelo and Sebastiano." The Borgherini Chapel was painted by Sebastiano using "designs" of Michelangelo. The same is true of other paintings in the show. Working at the dawn of the cult of the artist and the original reproduction, these two artists display an almost postmodern inventiveness when it comes to process, method, authorship, and result.

I visited Oxford on this trip to the United Kingdom, and while there I paid a visit to the Christ Church Picture Gallery. I asked if I might be permitted to take a photograph. No, I was told, but pencils could be provided if I wished to make my own reproductions.

This reminded me that the very idea of what it is to *make one's own reproduction*, or a copy, is now, as it was in Michelangelo's day, a moving target.

# 33 | WHO WAS VERMEER?

There are two excellent ideas at the heart of art historian Benjamin Binstock's beautiful and strange book *Vermeer's Family Secrets*. The first is taken from a Nietzsche quote: "We have learned to love all things that we now love."

The second is that you can't recognize a painting for what it is just by looking at it.[1] Getting to know, and so coming to love, a work of art, or the work of an artist, is itself hard work. Binstock compares it to bringing a distant planet into focus. It takes a lot of knowledge, and a great deal of careful attention to what others (scientists, historians, critics) have learned and thought, to be able to see what is out there.

Imagine a family. Father is a painter. Mother, the children, and also the maid are his models. Father works at home. The art changes and develops as his models grow up and as the relationships among them evolve. In time, one of his models, a child, takes up the brush and becomes the father's assistant and then his apprentice. The apprentice is confined, literally and figuratively, to the materials of the father—the same interior scenes, the same pigments, the same bolts of canvas. The apprentice seeks to imitate the master; but the master is also influenced, or even inspired, by the work of

125

the pupil, just as both of them share models because, after all, they share a single studio, home, and family.

This, Binstock claims, is exactly the situation in the Vermeer household. Scholars have long found it difficult to come up with a coherent story of Vermeer's development, or even of the order in which the very small number of extant paintings (some thirty-odd) were made. Some of the paintings just don't fit. They depict the same cast of characters occupying the same rooms and wearing the same clothes; they're made with the same paints using the same basic materials and techniques. But they *look* different. They lack the technical facility and compositional understanding of the others, even as they are also, sometimes, free-spirited and vigorous—worth loving!—in a way that is not typical of Vermeer.

Binstock is not alone in noticing that a good sixth of Vermeer's pictures don't seem to fit. He may be alone in advancing an account that explains not only their differences but also their similarities. Contrary to what has been widely supposed, Vermeer *did* have an apprentice: his daughter Maria (of pearl earring fame). And Binstock also offers plausible explanations of why it has taken until now for us to realize this. First, in the Delft of Vermeer's day, there was no requirement that children be registered as apprentices. Second, girls and women were not encouraged to paint, and Maria would have been expected, or perhaps required, to give up painting at marriage. Hence there is no sequel to her work in her father's studio. But finally, Vermeer's family paid the bills with the money from his paintings. Indeed, they traded paintings for food. Vermeer's widow deliberately passed off Maria's works as by the master himself in order to pay off debts. Maria, and to some degree Vermeer himself, were complicit in this. It was in everyone's interest to keep Maria's apprenticeship a secret. (As it was in their interest to keep other things secret, such as the family's illegal adherence to Catholicism.)

Contemporary scholars scoff at approaches to art that lean too heavily on cults of personality or biographical detail. After all, when work is good, it stands on its own and doesn't require a romantic backstory. Quite right. But Binstock makes the case that where Vermeer is concerned, the family *isn't* backstory. Vermeer painted his family. And his family painted right back.

Nor can Binstock be accused of making excuses for Vermeer, as if explaining away his bad paintings. Maria's paintings are very good. They are genuine artistic responses to the work of her father and, Binstock shows, they compelled her father to respond to them as works of art in turn, actively influencing his choices and development. She never equaled her father. But then her apprenticeship was very brief. It is truly extraordinary what she accomplished in a small number of years.

If Binstock is right, then seven paintings widely taken to be painted by Johannes Vermeer—and that fetch prices at auction in the millions of dollars—are not by his hand at all.

Which is of course not to say that these paintings are *not* Vermeers.

It would be wordplay to notice that they *are* by a Vermeer, after all: Maria Vermeer.

But the important and conceptually intriguing question raised by Binstock's book—and, if he is right, raised by Vermeer's oeuvre itself—is this: what is it to *be* a Vermeer, anyway?

In any event, millions of dollars hang in the balance. It will be very interesting to see how art history, as a field, responds to Binstock's (perhaps costly) challenge.

# 34 | HOW TO LOVE A FAKE

In 2013, a painting by Francis Bacon sold at Christie's for more than $142 million. At the time this was the most money ever paid for a single artwork at auction. The venerable New York art dealer Knoedler and Company shut its doors in 2011 in the face of legal charges that it had sold dozens of paintings purporting to be by Mark Rothko, Jackson Pollock, Willem de Kooning, and others that were actually counterfeits made by a man in a Queens garage. In 2014 a trove of art looted by the Nazis—hundreds of paintings—was found in an apartment in Munich.

Art stays in the news.

We sometimes think of paintings as like autographs. It's only Mick Jagger's autograph if he signed it with his very hand. And it's only a Vermeer, say, or a Rothko, if Vermeer or Rothko himself actually made the picture.

This makes good sense when it comes to autographs. A signature is a person's mark. By affixing our mark, we seal the deal; we make the commitment; we write the check. An autograph matters because it certifies.

But none of this is true of paintings. We value paintings for their own qualities. If we also admire the *painter*, this is only because he or she managed to make those objects whose value is otherwise manifest.

Perhaps, then, we should think of painting not on the autograph model but on what I'll call the architecture model. Le Corbusier doesn't have to have to build the structure with his own hands for it to be an expression of his artistic accomplishment. And so with painters. It isn't the dubious magic of the artist's touch that is significant. What matters, rather, is the distinct achievement of the artist's conception, a conception that can be realized in different ways.

This idea shouldn't be too strange. It is widely known that Titian, Rembrandt, Rubens, and other great masters ran workshops (factories) where assistants did significant portions of the actual labor. And no one seriously expects that Jeff Koons actually worked the stainless steel for *Balloon Dog Orange*, which in 2013 sold at auction for close to $60 million.

But there are borderline cases. Consider (as I discussed in Chapter 33) Benjamin Binstock's remarkable proposal that a number of Vermeer's paintings were probably made by his daughter, who had labored for a time as his apprentice. Let us suppose that Binstock is right. Does this mean that these Vermeers are not Vermeers, that they are fakes? Well, it means that they were not painted by him; he did not apply the paint to the canvas. On the autograph conception, they aren't Vermeers. But on the architectural conception, quite possibly (but not necessarily) they are. Maybe Vermeer found a new way to make paintings, a new method: he used his daughter!

This proposal has been advanced by the art critic Blake Gopnik. From Gopnik's standpoint (making a host of assumptions about the facts of the case), Vermeer's daughter's paintings *are* his paintings because they are the realization and working out of the father's project. It is an overly narrow and parochial conception of authorship—something like the autograph conception—that gets in the way of our appreciating that artists can do things, and make things, without actually doing them and making them.

Forgers, Gopnik proposes, and as I have already discussed in Chapter 30, can be an art lover's friend.[1]

Sometimes they give us works that great artists simply didn't get around to making. If a fake is good enough to fool experts, then it's good enough to give the rest of us pleasure, even insight.

Why suppose that a work is a fake or a copy just because the artist him- or herself didn't actually make it? What makes a fake a good one is that it realizes, or investigates, or approximates an artist's contribution. It makes a move in a space of possibilities opened up by him or her. It is the very fact of the forgery's success that ensures that what the forger is doing is relevant to the original artist's work and so, at least potentially, a contribution to it. Gopnik invites us to think of the faker as a kind of faithful assistant who just happened to arrive after the artist's death, or who set to work without the artist's explicit permission.

Gopnik's idea is an important one. It applies pressure to the idea that we know what it is for a painting to be a Vermeer or a Koons. Authorship, like the wider notion of agency itself, is fraught and delicate. And it is one of art's jobs to explore this.

Nevertheless, it is important to remember that in the real world we do not ever come up against forgeries that duplicate the qualities of their originals; we only ever come up against forgeries that seem to do this.

Yes, they may fool the experts, as Gopnik says. But only for now.

I don't mean to suggest that the experts will always get it right eventually, thanks to a kind of infallibility of expertise. Although there is actually something to this idea, not because experts are so smart, but rather because forgers usually deploy devices that are designed only to pull the wool over the eyes of the contemporary crowd; with the passage of time, significant stylistic difference emerges. (This familiar point was noted by Peter Schjeldahl in a somewhat unfriendly response to Gopnik in the *New Yorker*, as mentioned in Chapter 30.[2])

No, the deeper point is that we need to guard against misunderstanding what it means for an expert, or anyone else, to get it right.

Judgments in matters of art are themselves only ever works in progress, revising themselves in light of not only an ongoing engagement with the work but also a continuing dialogue with other artists and thinkers, past and present. What the art historian Meyer Schapiro called "critical seeing" is something we cultivate, spread out in time.[3] From that standpoint, getting fooled about what you are seeing needn't be a failure at all; it is, rather, a moment in an ongoing process.

Which takes us back to Gopnik's proposition. He's right that our engagement with a forgery can enable us to achieve insight into the work and conceptions of the artist who has been copied. But not because it fools the experts. Rather, it's precisely because, in time, it can't.

# 35 | MONUMENTS

We value works of art, whether by Leonardo da Vinci, Mark Rothko, or Rosie Lee Tompkins, for both personal and historical reasons.

Artworks are the products of an individual person's labor and the expression of this person's personality and style. Certain art may appeal to us individually.

Artworks also stand as historical evidence; they are artifacts of the conditions when and where they were put together. When an artwork is destroyed, not only do we lose our knowledge of an individual artist, but also our relation to the past is changed.

The reality is different, though, when it comes to monuments.

Monuments—as a general rule—obscure the conditions of their own production; they redirect our attention to the person or event they memorialize.

Observers don't generally view monuments while thinking about the artists. Do you know, for example, the name of the artist responsible for the Lincoln Memorial, or for the monument to Robert E. Lee in a park in Charlottesville, Virginia, that has been so controversial in recent years? Monuments are designed to direct our attention not back on the artist but to whatever it is the monuments are built to memorialize.

Monuments are often constructed years after said event happens or said hero lived. One might be surprised to learn that both the Lincoln Memorial and Charlottesville's monument to Robert E. Lee went up about sixty years after the end of the Civil War.

The curious thing about monuments, as Vanderbilt University art historian Matthew Worsnick told me, is that it is almost as if they "slip into an archival box; they are treated as if they were a kind of evidence or relic of their subjects."

When, of course, they aren't. Not really.

The memorials to Robert E. Lee and Lincoln are very much the product of their own time and place. The Civil War may have ended in 1865. But it is probably no accident that the Robert E. Lee statue in question went up in 1924, at the height of Jim Crow, two years after the dedication of the Lincoln Memorial.

But it is the distinct power of memorials—it is their point, really—that they obscure their partisan and parochial origins. In Worsnick's words: "Memorials often skew the timeline, they muddy the historical waters. They do this through a tendency to conceal the circumstances of their own production."

To destroy a Leonardo is to hurt Leonardo's legacy and to damage our grasp on his historical situation. But to destroy a monument to Robert E. Lee is to hurt *Lee's* legacy, not that of the responsible artist, and to alter our felt relation to Lee's time and place, rather than the time and place of the manufacture of his memorial.

There are all sorts of exceptions to these generalizations, and there may be all manner of ambiguities.

For example, the Vietnam Veterans Memorial, in Washington, DC, for all that it is a memorial, is actually very much associated with Maya Lin, its creator. And sometimes a memorial *is* truly a relic of that for which it stands as a memorial. Take, as an example, the Sarajevo Roses—scars created by mortar fire from the siege of 1992–1995 that were later filled in with red resin.

What is the upshot of these considerations for the ongoing debate about memorials to the Confederacy?

First, we must own up to the fact that the decision to let a monument stand—no less than the decision to take it down—is to take a stand on the subject matter of the monument. If you believe, as I do, that Robert E. Lee was a friend of slavery and an enemy of the United States of America, then the case for removing monuments to him is overwhelming.

Second, there is no reason to fear that tearing down such monuments will, or could, cause us to forget. The monuments are not and never have been relics of those bygone days. They carry no information about the past they are used to symbolize; all they tell us about is our own reverential attitude to that past. And that's a reverential attitude it is time to change, at least in this case.

Third, we must distinguish the objects—the actual statues—from their function as monuments. You can preserve the objects—the art and our felt relation to times past—without conserving their negative symbolic functions on public grounds. There are memorial parks in Moscow and Budapest, for example, where old Soviet monuments to Stalin and Lenin have been put on display. If you think there are good reasons to preserve these reminders of our national history—reminders of the fact that we once thought it useful to create the monument—this can be done without keeping them in force as monuments.

# PART IV

# Nature's Art

# 36 | AESTHETIC EVOLUTION

At the heart of Richard O. Prum's 2017 book *The Evolution of Beauty: How Darwin's Forgotten Theory of Mate Choice Shapes the Animal World—and Us* is a bold idea: "That animals are not merely subject to the extrinsic forces of ecological competition, predation, climate, geography, and so on that create natural selection. Rather, animals can play a distinct and vital role in their *own* evolution through their sexual and social choices."[1]

Actually, this is Darwin's idea, his *other* idea—an idea so revolutionary that, unlike natural selection itself, it has been systematically misunderstood, or outright repressed, since Darwin first developed it in his *other* book *The Descent of Man* (first published in 1871, twelve years after *The Origin of Species*).

What's so dangerous about what Prum calls "aesthetic evolution by mate choice"? Precisely the idea that it acknowledges real agency in the non-human world, and not only that, an agency that doesn't bottom out in facts about fitness and adaptation. Moreover, it does so, Prum argues, because it's good science.

Now, it isn't exactly news to be informed that Darwin grappled with the problem of the diversity, indeed the gorgeous magnificence, of ornament in the biological world. It is reported that he once wrote in a letter to a friend: "The sight of the feather in a peacock's tail, whenever I gaze at it, makes me sick!" For the peacock's tail is, manifestly, of no adaptive value whatsoever. It is no aid to flight, no benefit in combat with another, no enhancement of the ability to secure food or provide concealment from predators. In short, it would seem to be one of countless direct counterexamples to the proposition that biological traits are *adaptations*, that is, that they are selected to enhance survival value (or the ability to bring offspring into the world).

The thing about the peacock's tail is that the peahen *likes it*. It's sexy. It's beautiful to her. It is attractive. And that's why the peacock goes in for it, or rather, why peacocks who've got it and are able to flaunt it are in fact more likely to have offspring. So the trait is selected for not because of its adaptive value but by the female of the species.

And that, Prum suggests, is a radical idea, especially in Darwin's Victorian England, and even now, in a world where patriarchy is still the order of the day.

This is why, Prum argues, evolutionists have tended either to downplay sexual selection or to seek to ground it in the logic of adaptation. Perhaps the best-known strategy for doing this is to hold that the reason the peahen likes the peacock's tail is that the tail is actually a signal of the peacock's fitness: only a peacock from a good family with disposable income is going to live long enough to afford the luxury of maladaptive ornamentation. Ornament is conspicuous consumption, on this view, and females like it, so the reasoning goes, because they can't resist male power.

*Oy vey!* That is an ugly idea, and not one that casts the men who are its proponents in a particularly nice light.

According to Prum, it also completely misses Darwin's revolutionary idea: that the aesthetic delight animals take in each other—in this case, that females take in the males of the species——is *arbitrary*; it is grounded in nothing more than desire. The conscious sensory experience of animals—especially female animals—and the choices they make as a result of these experiences are one of the chief governing forces of natural evolution.

Now, Prum is an ornithologist, not a polemicist, and this book is a delight to read because of the knowledge, and also the love of learning and teaching, that it puts on display. On one point, though, I am quite certain he goes too far. In the final pages of the book he proposes to take his account of aesthetic evolution and use it to show that what the animals are doing and have been doing, and what Mozart, Manet, van Gogh, and Cézanne were doing, are all of a piece: art.

The basic problem with attempts to biologize art by grounding it in natural selection is that they end up treating art as like the peacock's tail—as just another form of conspicuous consumption. But whatever else is true, Mozart, Manet, and the rest are not bling; even if part of why we like them is that there is social prestige attached to them, it's just not very plausible that *that* is the basic source of their value.

But Prum's view, as we've already seen, is very different. As I have argued in a brief discussion of Prum in my book *Strange Tools*, in Prum's view beauty is the result of a *co*evolutionary process. "Changes in mating preferences have transformed the tail, and changes in the tail have transformed mating preferences," Prum writes, and he extends this account to human art. According to Prum, the pleasures we take in art are directly and specifically bound up with art. Not because art generates a special sort of aesthetic feeling or sensation. But because our responses to art—the pleasures we take in it—are bound up with art itself by processes of coevolution. What we like shapes art, and art, in turn, shapes and reshapes what we like. Art, like attractive ornament in the biological world, is the result of coevolutionary processes spanning evolutionary and cultural time scales. Art, as Prum puts it, is "a form of communication that co-evolves with its own evolution" One of the strengths of this view is that it can do justice to radical change in aesthetic evaluation. The works of an artist—think of those of Andy Warhol, for example—can *become* beautiful, for these works can contribute to the changing of the very criteria of evaluation by which we aesthetically assess this work itself. And Prum's account also does justice to the fact that it is one thing to like something, and another to find it beautiful. Beauty—finding something aesthetically pleasing—isn't just a matter of liking it. For Prum can allow that our pleasures and preferences get refined through evolutionary recursion. Some pleasures—like the pleasures we might take in an elegant mathematical proof, for example, or in the work of Beethoven—are only available to those who stand on the scaffolding of past communication and agreements.

This is a very powerful proposal. It brings out the distinctively *cognitive*—that is to say, *evaluative*—character of the pleasures that art affords. We don't just respond to art; we *judge* it.

Now, I don't doubt for a minute that peahens take pleasure in what they see when they see a handsome peacock. Indeed, the seeing itself gives them pleasure. And I have no objection to calling that pleasure aesthetic.

But is it really true that when we look at a work of art we enjoy pleasures of *that* kind? Not all art is "aesthetic" in this sense. And I don't just mean Warhol and Duchamp, or even Beethoven's late string quartets. The experience of art is seldom tied, in the way the peahen's gaze is tied, to lust or desire for what you are looking at. I may take pleasure when I gaze upon a Poussin landscape, but it is a pleasure that is in no way tied to the actual presence of the figures depicted inside the painting. And when Mozart's audiences delighted in the ways he foiled their expectations of how a piece of music was supposed to be organized, they were getting his joke, understanding his thought, not just languishing in pleasurable sounds.

But I also fear that Prum's theory, as a theory of art, ends up casting the net too wide: every artifact or social activity or technology is constrained by what we like (evaluative response) even as it offers the opportunity for us to change and update those responses (coevolution). Art is not merely a social activity or technology even if it masquerades as such. For art always disrupts business as normal and puts on display the fact that we find ourselves carrying out business as normal. Put bluntly: the value of art consists not in a (coevolving) fit (or dialog) between what we make and what we like, but rather in the practice of investigating and questioning and challenging such processes.

I met Prum once, a few years before his book's publication. He heard me give a lecture and we sat next to each other discussing these questions at dinner afterward. It was a delightful encounter. I fear, however, that he might have had me, or at least those like me, in mind when he writes: "Some aesthetic philosophers, art historians, and artists may find the recognition of myriad new biotic art forms to be more of an annoyance, or even an outrage, than a contribution to their fields." Maybe so. But, speaking for myself anyway, it's not because I doubt the aesthetic richness of the natural world. Or because I see reason to deny the importance of the experience of pleasure and, indeed, of something like beauty on the part of animals. Animals are truly, in Prum's sense, aesthetic agents.

The problem is not with Prum's insistence that we say yes to the aesthetic lives of animals; I applaud that. The problem is that, as I read him, Prum ends up saying no to art.

# 37 | BOWIE, CHEESECAKE, SEX, AND THE MEANING OF MUSIC

When David Bowie released "Where Are We Now?" back in 2013, I found myself observing: The song is new, but it sounds old. It sounds familiar. It sounds like a David Bowie song. It is new and familiar at the same time. This is, in part, I think, what makes it so good.

This got me thinking about the fact that music has a history. This is puzzling. Why *should* music have a history?

Bowie's music was once new. Now it's not, even when it is. My young son wouldn't be drawn to a song by Bowie as he would be to a song by Jay-Z. Jay-Z is of the now. Bowie is not, even when he is. What is this about?

According to cognitive psychologist Steven Pinker, music is like cheesecake.[1] We don't have a cheesecake faculty. We are not designed by evolution to appreciate cheesecake. It is our appreciation of fat and sugar, rather, that is adaptive. Cheesecake is simply a well-optimized fat and sugar delivery system. NYU psychologist Gary Marcus agrees with the music as auditory cheesecake view. Music, he adds, is a refined craft for tickling the brain by acting on reward systems sensitive to repetition and novelty.[2]

Does this help us understand why music has a history? Cheesecake doesn't have a history. Not really. I bet my grandma's cheesecake is *better* than anything I might find today. Not so when it comes to music. We crave the new. And each generation craves *its* new music.

The cheesecake theory of music treats music as like a species of masturbation. Masturbation has no history. The good that it delivers is unchanging; it is perfect as it is. And for the simple reason that the mechanics of orgasm are fixed by our basic body plan.

To this it will be objected: the pleasures induced by fat, sugar, and orgasm may be stable, but the means available to us for achieving these ends—the techniques, practices, technologies, and perversions—are indeed always evolving, and with the same rapidity, and so history, as in any other area of technology (transportation, communication, etc.).

Music, from this standpoint, is an evolving technology for auto-titillation and reward. Change in music is technological change. Not change in what we like. But change in how we get it. (I think this is Marcus's view.)

This approach doesn't quite hit the nail on the head. The problem is not merely that music changes over time; it's that what we like, what moves us, interests us, and seems relevant to us changes as well. Why should that be?

The problem with the cheesecake/masturbation theory of music is that it reduces music to mere psychological cause and effect. As if the value of a song is exhausted by its psychological action on a person! Music may give us pleasure, just as sex does, but neither sex nor music is primarily in the titillation business.

Here's a better idea: compare a song to a conversation. A conversation unfolds. It captures the interest of its participants. Sometimes one person talks, sometimes another. The conversation is dynamic. It is also embedded in a situation and unfolds against a background. People aren't just jibber-jabbering (to use a word that was briefly trendy). They are talking *about* something, paying attention jointly to a problem, amusing themselves, or having fun, as the case may be. In some ways a conversation is constantly changing. In other ways it is always the same, just people talking. Are some conversations better than others? Yes, certainly. But is the conversation of one generation or one epoch better than another? That barely makes sense.

And yet conversation is always of the now. Not because new technologies are getting deployed in new ways to make better conversational repartee. But because our thoughts, interests, concerns, are contemporary. Music, like conversation, doesn't get old in the sense that the intrinsic quality or character of music changes. It simply ceases to be a response to what people are saying, doing, or thinking about now.

And this explains something else. It is the distinctive limitation of the juvenile perspective or of the novice listener (whether to conversation or to music) to be stuck with the present and the new. They only join the conversation now, after all. For the adult listener, though, the new is a passage into the past—background, history—and then at once a way into a future that only now comes into view.

# 38 | DYLAN'S LITERATURE

The announcement that Bob Dylan would be awarded the 2016 Nobel Prize in Literature was not the most surprising and unanticipated event in public life that year. That prize surely goes to the election to the US presidency of a man entirely unqualified for the job who was previously known for his reality TV appearances rather than for his intellect, skill in business, or interest in politics or public service.

But Dylan's prize was wildly unanticipated nonetheless; in fact, it was a shocking and vaguely disorienting occurrence, a cause for celebration, perhaps, but also, like Trump's victory, something almost unthinkable. It isn't just that Dylan's prize registers a changing of the guard. It is that, like Trump's presidency, it can seem almost like a sort of category mistake. Trump isn't a politician, not really. And Dylan's a rock star, or a folk singer, or a pop musician. He's not a writer, neither of fiction nor of poetry or drama. Pop music and literature are as different from each other as painting is from filmmaking. Dylan, you might think, no more deserves a literature prize than Warhol deserves an Academy Award. (Which is not to say that Dylan and Warhol are not great artists.)

Dylan himself takes on the question of his relation to literature in his Nobel Prize lecture—deadpan, just perceptibly ironic, but touching for all that—which has been published in the form of a recording. His treatment of the question is, in a way, straightforward. He's a musician, he explains, whose vernacular is that of the folk singer. As a young person in grammar school, he read many great books, and some of them impressed him deeply. He offers a detailed and rather impassioned account of a few of these: a scorching description of *All Quiet on the Western Front*, a moving and humane précis of *The Odyssey*, and a dazzling synopsis of *Moby Dick*. Dylan doesn't have a lot to say specifically about how these books influenced his work. In fact, he handles that question rather like a grammar school student. He asserts, blandly, that he engages themes from these books in his own songs ("Ishmael survives. He's in the sea floating on a coffin. And that's about it. That's the whole story. That theme and all that it implies would work its way into more than a few of my songs").

But this is only a pretend simplemindedness, I think. It is the *way* that Dylan describes the books he remembers and loves—the way he sings their praises and intones feelings, emotions, images; the energy with which he acknowledges allegory and reference— that suggests to the listener that he and the authors of these books are indeed caught up in the same project of telling stories, weaving images, and building skeins of verbal pictures and statement. And that's the project of literature.

But just when you think he's *showing* you that he deserves the literature prize after all, he throws a curveball. Songs are made for singing, he says. They don't live on the page. "Our songs are alive in the land of the living. But songs are unlike literature. They're meant to be sung, not read." The thought seems to be that his songs are not to be confused with text-based literature. So maybe his real point is that he's not a literary artist?

But not so fast! He doesn't let us rest easy with that conclusion either, since he adds right away that songs are made for singing the way Shakespeare's lines are made to be performed onstage: "The words in Shakespeare's plays were meant to be acted on the stage. Just as lyrics in songs are meant to be sung, not read on a page." So if Shakespeare's genre is a literary one, then so, it would seem, is Dylan's.

Finally, Dylan's lecture—which is read with theatrical emphasis and a singsong quality to a musical accompaniment—does what the best art (and also the best philosophy) always does: it uncovers hidden questions and throws certainties into doubt. What is literature anyway? What is song? What is art?

# 39 | WHAT'S NEW IS OLD

Plagiarism is passing off someone else's work as your own. It is an act of deception. Not every failure to fully disclose my background, feelings, sources, or inspiration is deceptive. For not every failure to disclose will invite you falsely to understand who I am and what I am doing. Deception, like any communicative act, requires very special stage-setting.

It's useful to remember this when considering charges of plagiarism leveled against Bob Dylan and Beyoncé. In both cases, the accusations strike me as misguided (which is not to say that intellectual property rights may not be at stake; that's a separate matter).

As art critic Blake Gopnik, writing in *Newsweek*, reminds us in connection with the Dylan case, painters as diverse as Degas, Matisse, Warhol, and Richter have made use of unnamed photographs in their painting practices. Dylan is just participating in what is really a common practice in modern painting. Complaining that the images derive from pictures is a bit like complaining that an artist's finished product resembles the real people he used as models in the studio.

There is also a deeper point: painting as an art is always, up front and on its surface, concerned with precisely the question of painting as a medium. This is not a recent thing. Some people worship painted icons. Others insist that to do so is heresy; a picture, after all, is never more than a trifling product of earthbound handicraft. What is a painted picture by an artist? And what is its relation to its "prototype"? Contemporary artists continue to grapple with these issues endlessly. (Consider, for example, Hiroshi Sugimoto's photographic remaking of Holbein paintings.)

Painting, and art in general, has its own distinct communicative setting, and the idea that Dylan can be accused of deception, or plagiarism, in that context is downright silly. We need to look elsewhere—and I suspect we don't have far to look—if we want to criticize his painting.

The Beyoncé case is more delicate, if only because "Countdown" is a pop music video likely to be seen millions of times over by people who have no clue that she liberally samples from *Rosas danst Rosas*, a work by Anne Teresa De Keersmaeker, a major Belgian choreographer (or rather, that she borrows from a dance-for-film version of De Keersmaeker's work by the Belgian filmmaker Thierry de Mey). It is difficult not to consider this case in the light of the fact that dance—even in Europe, where funding is much better than it is here—tends to be non-commercial and for that reason culturally marginal.

You can sympathize with the choreographer, who may simply want the acknowledgment that *she* has been seen, that her work is noticed. De Keersmaeker is quoted in the *Guardian* as saying: "What's rude is that they don't even bother about hiding it. They seem to think they could do it because it's a famous work. . . . Am I honoured? Look I've seen local school kids doing this. That's a lot more beautiful."[1]

One thing is clear: no one could watch Beyoncé's video carefully and not see that the scenes that directly refer to De Keersmaeker arrive with quotation marks around them. The phrases from De Keersmaeker and de Mey are inserted (sampled) as if from another artistic landscape into the very different space that Beyoncé and her dancers have been occupying; there is something even flashback-like about the sequences, as though Beyoncé's persona is harking back to her own dance-school background.

It is because *Rosas danst Rosas* has a life and importance outside the context of its performance by De Keersmaeker's company in Belgium that it can serve unnamed, as it does for Beyoncé, as part of the streaming background for her own imaginative play.

It's also worth noticing that Beyoncé's engagement with dance and its history is long-standing. Her video for "Single Ladies"— surely one the best pop music videos *ever*—is replete with references to the steps of Bob Fosse, as well as to classical dance, as choreographer William Forsythe once explained to me. Dance and its history provide an imagescape against which Beyoncé does her thing.

Does Beyonce's exemplification of De Keersmaeker's ideas enhance their value or diminish them? Is there a legal case to be made here? I leave that to the legal experts. But about this question there can be no doubt: Beyoncé did nothing genuinely fraudulent.

But our discussion cannot end here. Anxieties about plagiarism can seem to have a new urgency in our era in which ideas, images, thoughts, and inventions are so easily reduced to data strings that can be transmitted, reproduced, and manipulated with little cost and effort. "Sampling" is the word we now use to refer to the practices of assembling and recombining words, song, and movement of others in new ways to make something new out of something old.

Sampling is nothing new, not in art and not in life. Every time you use a word or phrase you are, wittingly or not, making a pastiche out of the linguistic gestures of those who came before you. Evolution, whether in biology or in technology and culture, is never anything other than a redeployment of old means in new circumstances. We use the old to make the new, and the new is always old.

In the absence of direct intention to deceive, plagiarism has nothing to do with this.

Anne Teresa de Keersmaeker surely got the last laugh when, in 2013, she launched the Fabulous Rosas Remix Project, an international call to the general public to learn the Rosas and share video on de Keersmaeker's own web site (rosasdanstosas.be). As of August 2021, there are 664 filmed dance performances posted online, not one of which, I would venture, is an act of plagiarism.

# 40 | THE PERFORMANCE ART OF DAVID BOWIE: A REMEMBRANCE

In jazz and classical music, the performance, live or recorded, is a vehicle for the music; it's the music that matters. This is not the case with pop music. When it comes to pop music, it's the other way around: the music, always more or less accessible, more or less recognizable, is a vehicle for the performer, or at least for an idea of the performer. This is why pop music, although *musical*, is always also a spectacle. The music is a spotlight that shines bright on the person or persons who are, as it were, *in person*, the real art.

Pop music is performance art. We find examples of this early on in the history of pop music. Think of the nearly mythological character of Robert Johnson, or the nearly equally mythologized Hank Williams. The critic Dave Hickey, as I discussed in *Strange Tools*, wrote an essay about Williams that perfectly captures him, indicates what he's about artistically, but does so in a way that fails to discuss his music in any detail. The focus instead is sex, drugs, and a life on the road.

But it is since the sixties that pop music, as an art form, has really acquired its characteristic shape. It is the death of David Bowie in January 2016, one of its greatest proponents—indeed, one of its inventors—that occasions this remembrance. He is a great artist the way Andy Warhol is a great artist. And they are performance artists both. Warhol has about as much to do with painting (or *visual* art), really, as Bowie has to do with music. Which is to say *everything*, but in some ways also nothing. Warhol used visual art as a vehicle to make art in the medium of himself, and the same is true of Bowie and music. Even their names, as is the case with their artistic soul mate Bob Dylan, are made up.

And this explains why it is that in the vast outpouring of admiration and mourning for Bowie, both by critics and by fans, both in the press and on social media, there has been barely a word devoted to Bowie's *music*.

Hilton Als, writing in the *New Yorker*, has described Bowie's generosity to other artists such as Iggy Pop and Ava Cherry. He writes: "Bowie called it [his song 'Young Americans'] 'plastic soul,' which was an honest thought. Bowie was not a soul man; he was borrowing from soul artists—the guys who made the sound of Philadelphia just that—in order to make his new self, backed by incredible black artists like Ava Cherry and Luther Vandross."[1] That's about as close as Als gets to discussing a musical idea. Composition, timbre, innovation, melody, instrumentation, technology, methods of recording—these go pretty much unmentioned here, as they also do in Ben Ratliff's survey of Bowie's greatest songs in the *New York Times*.[2] Ratliff's descriptions of the songs make reference to "overdriven guitars" or "strummier" songs, but this hardly rises to the level of specific engagement with musical ideas or qualities.

If I'm right, there's no fault here, not on the part of Ratliff, Als, or anyone else. When it comes to Bowie's music, or that of other great rock or pop artists, it just isn't about the music; it never was. Als is spot on when he puts emphasis on *the position* Bowie takes up in relation to soul, or on his actual literal position on the stage as Bowie plays keyboard behind Iggy Pop on *The Dinah Shore Show*. When it comes to Bowie—and this is true of all the great pop stars (a few at random: John Lennon, Kanye West, David Byrne, Michael Stipe, Patti Smith, Mick Jagger, Bob Dylan, and I would add Andy Warhol)—it's almost always primarily about the position, the stance, the attitude, the style.

Ratliff expresses some disagreement with me about the music in pop music,[3] but I am struck that his actual critical practice fits my account perfectly. And when he says that Bowie took the question of image and identity seriously, he is actually, I think, putting his finger on a defining attitude of pop music.

Actually, there has been tons of discussion in print and online about Bowie's lyrics, and surely the lyrics belong to the music, so it isn't entirely right to say the music is neglected. Ratliff, for example, is persuasive when he demonstrates that shifts in the moods of Bowie's work over time show up in the words of his songs. And Simon Critchley, writing in *The New York Times*, to give another example, discusses the significance of the frequent occurrence of the word "nothing" in Bowie's songs.[4]

But the very great bulk of what has been written about Bowie has focused not on the music proper but on the astonishing transformations in Bowie's appearance through the years, on his changing styles in both dress and sound, on his steady and playful reinvention, and, above all else, on his androgyny and other aspects of his perceived sexuality. As one brilliant gay friend of mine, writing on Facebook, put it: "Bowie . . . was our extraterrestrial,

our outsider, our gorgeous bookish androgynous super freak."
And others I've bumped into online write about what it meant
to them growing up to know that Bowie was . . . well, that Bowie
was *a possibility*. Critchley, who is a philosopher and the author of
a book on Bowie as well as a fan, writes in the same *Times* article:

> For the hundreds of thousands of ordinary working-class
> boys and girls in England in the early 1970s, including me,
> Bowie incarnated something glamorous, enticing, exciting
> and mysterious: a world of unknown pleasures and sparkling
> intelligence. He offered an escape route from the suburban
> hellholes that we inhabited. Bowie spoke most eloquently to
> the disaffected, to those who didn't feel right in their skin, the
> socially awkward, the alienated. He spoke to the weirdos, the
> freaks, the outsiders and drew us in to an extraordinary inti-
> macy, although we knew this was total fantasy.

David Bowie's achievement as an artist, like Warhol's, is (still)
distinctively contemporary. Indeed, it may be more distinctively
"relevant" than that of Ellsworth Kelly and Pierre Boulez, two
other hugely influential and admired artists, both of whom died
around the same time Bowie did. And one measure of this may be
the fact that even today, almost thirty years after Warhol's death,
and in the aftermath of David Bowie's all too early demise, we can
still hardly say what it is that they were doing. We don't really have
a name for it. Warhol was not a painter or visual artist (the way
Rembrandt or de Kooning was), and Bowie is not a musician (in
the same sense as Beethoven or Charles Mingus).

# 41 | ALL THINGS SHINING

In Ridley Scott's movie *Blade Runner*, Deckard (played by Harrison Ford) is a blade runner, a cop charged with capturing rebel androids (replicants). To find out whether a suspected replicant *is* a replicant, he deploys a sort of lie-detector test: he poses emotionally loaded questions to would-be replicants and uses a device to measure a telltale physiological response.

Deckard's hard-cop detachment is deeply incompatible with the kinds of relationships—even romantic ones—that he himself carries on with replicants. This brings us to the argument of the movie: in treating others as if a physiological response is called for to decide if they count or not—in taking up a detached attitude that is willing to call their very humanity into question—Deckard convincingly puts his own humanity in jeopardy. This is driven home when we learn that Deckard himself, unbeknownst to him, may be a replicant.

Although Hubert Dreyfus and Sean Kelly don't discuss *Blade Runner* in their important book *All Things Shining*, they might have. Deckard's is just the sort of perversion they investigate.[1]

Physicists Stephen Hawking and Leonard Mlodinow, in their book *The Grand Design*, suggest that the Greek gods, like all gods, were posits of ignorant people to explain phenomena they didn't

159

understand.[2] *All Things Shining* offers a *very* different picture. Homer's gods stand for meanings in the world around us, and also for the moods or moments when we are most drawn to or sensitive to those meanings. Aphrodite, for example, marks the untrammeled power of erotic love, a force that can be overwhelming when one is in the right mood.

Homer doesn't suggest that the goddess actually causes lust! The point, rather, is that erotic love is not something we decide to find compelling. It confronts us with full force. And then there's this: it isn't easy to be open to the full force of things, not erotic love, not anything else. This is why Helen, who abandons her husband and infant to run off with Paris, eventuating in the Trojan War and terrible suffering, is celebrated in Homer as no less a hero than Odysseus himself. She allows herself to be open to one of life's unstoppable forces.

We can find this sort of openness to the living values in the world around us everywhere, in the large and in the small. Think of the way a soldier is drawn to perform a great deed. He may not *decide* to be brave. He just acts. Or think of the way a skilled craftsperson handles tools and materials. In cases such as this, skillful attunement to what a situation requires takes over. No need for contemplation. It is as if a god carries us along.

Neither Homer nor Dreyfus and Kelly are recommending that we abandon our families to chase sexual satisfaction. Nor do Dreyfus and Kelly naively suppose that all ancient Greeks led meaningful and intense lives. A successful openness to what calls, after all, is not something any of us get for free. It is a blessing of the gods, available to slave and free person alike.

Unless we actively resist it. Which, in a way, is the besetting sin of the modern age. Our nihilism comes *before* skepticism about God (or gods). It arises from the fact that we position ourselves before the world as if we were new arrivals who are in charge of our own agendas. We stand back and apart and try to figure out what we should believe, what we should value, what kind of people we should be. In our earnest, hyperintellectualized thoughtfulness, we are like Deckard in *Blade Runner*, so alienated from what really matters that we think we need a test to find out who (or what) is real.

Indeed, this has been a central commitment of main swaths of modern philosophy. To be a human being is to be a legislator; or perhaps it is to be a fact-finder and policy wonk.

Suppose two ships are sinking and you can only save one. Sound reason dictates that you save the ship with the most people in it.

But when this question was put by her hardheaded teacher to Sissy Jupe, the young girl in Charles Dickens's *Hard Times*, she could only burst into tears and run away. Sissy was unable to take up the standpoint from which this question could even be asked. For to take up this standpoint is already to have become blind—as Deckard is blind—to life shining, to its sacredness.

Dreyfus and Kelly don't argue that we should return to Homeric values. But they warn us not only of the dangers of our hubris but of its basic incoherence. We cannot decide what moves us.

# 42 | YOU SAY "TOMATO"

My dad speaks with a German accent. Or so I am told. I can't hear it. Nothing unusual about that. But this is an instance of a very important yet poorly understand human phenomenon: the Variation Effect (as I'll call it).

To bring the Variation Effect into focus, consider some examples.

How does one pronounce the word *Thursday*? Well, they do it one way in London's cockney East End and a different way in Afro-Caribbean Brixton. Different pronunciations abound in Brisbane, Brooklyn, Asheville, and Vancouver. There is no one way to say *Thursday*, or any other word, for that matter.

Variety occurs not only at the level of regions and populations. The next time you are at a table with friends, sitting at a bar, or in a shop, pay attention to the way people talk. You'll notice surprising variation in inflection, emphasis, contraction, rhythm, melody, volume, timbre, et cetera.

In fact, it's variation all the way down, even at the level of the individual. You choose your words and articulate your speech one way when you're talking to an elderly man in the nursing home, another way when you're addressing students from the podium, a third when you're discussing the quarterback's performance with other fans at the stadium. What counts as stylish, thoughtful, polite, sensitive, respectful, funny, or generous varies from one setting to another, depending on, among other things, to whom you are talking, whether the conversation is professional, and so on. It is a mark of either stupidity or arrogance to be unable or unwilling to accommodate one's manner of speech to the circumstances in which one finds oneself.

As variation plays a central role in biological evolution, it also plays a fascinating role in the evolution of languages, as Guy Deutscher tells in his delightful book *The Unfolding of Language*.[1]

Consider: The French say *pied*, whereas we say *foot*. They say *père*, where we say *father*. To our *for*, they have *pour*, and where we say *first*, they say *premier*. Systematically there is a correspondence between words with *p* sounds in French and words with *f* sounds in English. What explains this, say historians of language, is that the French and English languages descend from a common ancestor. For various reasons French, but not English, preserves the more ancient *p*-sound pronunciations that would have been used in this ancestral tongue. At some point in the last four hundred years or so, speakers of languages such as English, German, and Danish, but not speakers of French, Italian, and Spanish, started to say *f*, whereas earlier we said *p*.

How did this transition happen? What's remarkable is that the change goes unmentioned in the historical record. How can this be? First, how can people have failed to notice and remark on a steady, systematic change in the way people talk? And second, how could they have failed to shut it down? Speakers love to criticize mispronunciation, and surely that's what saying *f* for *p* would have sounded like: a big error!

One hypothesis is that the change was imperceptible because it was gradual. As Deutscher explains, leading linguists as recently as the middle of the last century thought this gradual-change thesis was plausible. But it isn't. It's ludicrous. As Deutscher remarks, there's *p*, there's *pf*, and there's *f*. How is gradual change supposed to mask those contrasts? You can hear the difference, can't you?

Some ideas are beautiful, and the explanation Deutscher offers is very beautiful indeed. The very question—why didn't people notice the sound change when it happened?—relies on the tacit assumption that there was ever a single way people pronounced the words in question. But there is no one way to pronounce these words or any other. The ground of linguistic reality is comprehensible variation. And so there never was a single or unified sound change.

Then what happened? All there is and ever was is variation, but what does change over time is the frequency of different forms or pronunciations across the field of variations. People didn't change the way they talked. What changed was the number of people who talked one way relative to those who talked another.

And this explains why we didn't notice the sound change. This is an example of the Variation Effect. We have a great facility to adapt to, accommodate, and ignore variation.

Did you notice when *bad*, in the mouths of certain speakers, starting meaning "good," or, to go even farther back, when *cool* started to mean "stylish" and "positive"? I hear my student describe a book as "sweet" and I know he means something very different from what my mother would mean if she were to describe the very same book as "sweet." We are fluent and adaptable when it comes to different ways of talking here and now, and so we are not nonplussed by changes in the frequency distribution of different ways of talking. Meaning changes are not one-off occurrences, like heart attacks. They are gradual shifts in the behavior of lots of people against a background of unceasing variation.

Or consider a visual example: What does this tomato look like? Well, it looks one way from up close, when I hold it in my hand. It looks entirely different when I look at it from across the room, or when it is sitting on a pile of two hundred tomatoes in the grocery store. Likewise, its color looks one way under the store's fluorescent overheads and entirely different in daylight, or in the yellow tungsten lighting in the kitchen at home.

How does it *really* look? There's no such thing.

The point is not that the tomato isn't really red, or that there isn't in fact a single word *Thursday*. It's that to perceive entities or properties such as these is to be knowledgeably or skillfully sensitive to patterns or structures of variation—to the ways how things look, or how words sound, predictably change as circumstances change.

To perceive a word is to perceive something that is, of its basic nature, open to varieties of ways of showing up. A word that could only be pronounced one way (by one person? on a single occasion?) would not be a word at all. And to perceive a colored object is to understand—practically, not intellectually—that how it looks would vary in reliable ways were the lighting or one's angle of viewing to change. That's just what it is to have a certain color. It's to be a locus of possible visual variation of a certain style.

To perceive or cognize the world at all is to be sensitive to the way patterns of variation allow for invariance to show up for us. We achieve access to that which is invariant (the color, the word) not because we are blind to variation but because we are so fluent in our mastery of variation that we can let it recede for us and rest in the background.

In these ways we come to appreciate that perception is at bottom an aesthetic achievement.

# 43 | WHAT IS A FACT?

When I was in ninth grade or so, we were having a debate in one of my classes. I can't remember what it was about. One of my close friends produced a statistic that decisively brought the debate to a close. His side won. The statistic was decisive; the facts just spoke for themselves. Later on I asked him how it was he'd known that statistic, how he'd managed to have it at his fingertips. I was impressed by his reply. "I just made it up," he said.

He was my punk rock buddy; when we weren't absorbing the attitudes and music of the Ramones and the Sex Pistols, we were reading literature by Camus and Kafka. So how could I fail to be impressed by his irreverence, by his cleverness? But I was shocked too. He had lied!

I was put in mind of this when I read John D'Agata and Jim Fingal's 2012 book *The Lifespan of a Fact*. D'Agata is an essayist; Fingal is a much younger man who had been hired by *The Believer* as a fact-checker to review one of D'Agata's essays for publication. Fingal ended up writing more than a hundred pages' worth of corrections on D'Agata's essay. D'Agata wasn't having any of it; he defended his facts and his choices. He gave up in the end, though; the version of the essay that appeared in *The Believer* was a fact-checked *corrected* version. *The Lifespan of a Fact* is a book they put together after the dust settled; it's a reconstruction of the exchanges, or really their battle, as they work their way line by line through the original essay. But what makes the book remarkable is that it is, really, a kind of staging—after the manner of Plato, as journalist and author Lawrence Weschler observed to me in conversation—of an investigation into such questions as: What is a fact? What is the truth? When is it okay, for the sake of a good story, to simplify, change, or color facts? Is it possible to tell a story without doing so? Are there different demands in different genres of so-called non-fiction writing—literary essays, for example, or straight reporting? Can one even draw a sharp line between fiction and non-fiction? Can there be objectivity?

Instead of taking up this issue directly here, I thought I'd return to the anecdote with which I began. You see, the thing is, now that I stop to think about it, I wasn't exactly accurate with the story. It all happened exactly as I reported. My friend really did trot out the statistics. But it wasn't in *my* class. I wasn't actually there. I heard about it afterward. Indeed, I heard about it from the teacher of that other class, whom I knew rather well and who was a very reliable source. It was she who'd asked him how he'd known the statistics; she later reported back to me his startling answer.

Did I lie? Was my writing fraudulent? What should a good fact-checker say?

I am pulled in different directions. Yes, I did misrepresent the facts. But I didn't misrepresent any of the facts that mattered for what I was talking about. My friend really did misuse statistics in this way. We really were existential-philosophy-reading fourteen-year-old punk rockers, and we really were friends. I just simplified for the sake of the story, and in part because I didn't want to have to explain why it is that a *teacher* was talking to me frankly about my friend, a fellow pupil. (She was the mother of my girlfriend; we were friends. She admired my friend and told the story beaming with pride for what she felt was a good-spirited intellectual playfulness; I wasn't so sure.) But all of this, it seemed to me, was beside the point. The point, after all, was just that some people are willing to misrepresent the facts to win an argument or achieve an effect, and that this is questionable.

And then there's this. Did I *knowingly* misrepresent the facts? Well, yes, but then, not exactly. It's not as though I thought, "Well, here's what happened, but it's a bit cumbersome to report; I can make a better story if I just change the facts a little bit." What actually happened was that the improved story just sort of tripped off my tongue (or out of my typing fingers) *as if it were the truth.* But isn't this just as bad? Is a lazy indifference to the truth, is being seduced into believing one's own distortions, any better than an outright lie? How do we adjudicate these questions?

But now hang on and consider this: Suppose I told you—I am not saying this, just suppose—that actually *I* am the one who won the debate by lying. Suppose I told the story in the way that I did not so much because I didn't want to incriminate myself (after all these years, who cares?) but because if I were to admit that *I* had been the one lying, then the story would be about me, when what I wanted to open up for consideration was something that has nothing to do with me. What would you say then? Would this tend to mitigate, in your mind, the importance of my misrepresentations, or would it make them worse?

We only make statements, report facts, describe events, in shared communicative contexts. And these contexts come in many shapes, sizes, and qualities. I never felt lied to by President Clinton when he insisted that he'd "never had sex with that woman." This is because, as a general rule, I don't expect people to be truthful about such things, at least not in that sort of public setting. I confess to having a similarly tolerant attitude to Mike Daisey, the performance artist whose 2012 *This American Life* monolog about his visits to factories in China where Apple products are produced turned out to have factual inaccuracies. Ira Glass, whose radio show *This American Life* is not a news program but a storytelling hour, was horrified to learn that one of his storytellers had taken factual liberties. But Glass's outrage has always seemed inappropriate, even silly, to me. Granted, the fact-checking at *This American Life* falls short of today's fact-based journalism standards; it wouldn't have cut it at *All Things Considered* or the *New Yorker*. But isn't this a good thing? Aren't there different kinds of storytelling? Different kinds of non-fiction? And correspondingly different critical demands placed on readers and hearers? And anyway, none of this has any bearing on *the truth* or at least the importance of Daisey's assertion that workers in China's high-technology factories suffer appalling conditions and that this is something that we, as consumers, ought to care about. There are two sides to this question, of course. But they don't really turn on the sort of factual mistakes or distortions (which were they?) made by Daisey.

I saw a movie the other day that began with a text screen: "This is based on a true story. Only the facts have been changed." Sometimes, it seems to me, that gets it about right.

# 44 | STREAMS OF MEMES

A few years ago, my son, then probably about eleven years old, showed me a stupid little captioned photo that he'd found online; he referred to it as a meme.

I explained that he was misusing that word. The concept of a meme was introduced by Richard Dawkins and then developed by Daniel Dennett and Susan Blackmore. A meme, according to these scholars, is the cultural analog of a gene; like genes, memes spread, and in their spreading they take on a life of their own. Genes make up organisms, and memes make up cultural agglomerations of organisms. Cultural evolution moves faster than biological evolution and in some respects defies it; for example, cultural evolution can be Lamarckian (acquired characteristics can be passed on down the line). But culture, so necessary to human life, is subject, like biology itself, to evolutionary forces, to design without a designer, and to the emergence of novelty and diversification.

Well, it turns out—as you know—that my son was correct in his use of the term *meme*. He was doubly correct, actually. He was aware, as I was not, that the term had acquired a new meaning and was now used to refer precisely to just the sort of ironic Hallmark-card-esque image/word mock-up that he'd shown me. But on top of that, memes, in the new internet social media sense, *are* memes in the sense of Dawkins and company. Not exactly the most profound, life-changing ones, to be sure, but nevertheless contagious, lively, and evolving through iterations and reiterations not subject to anyone's control.

Actually, memes are memes not so much in the ways that technologies such as the wheel, fire, cars, toasters, and email are. Rather, memes are the stuff of jokes, satire, wit, and—most generally—art. Even the application of the term *meme* to refer to such silly, humble, low-bandwidth bits of ephemera is the sort of ironic appropriation that sheds light and offers insight, at least potentially.

Memes are really a lot like jokes, as another twelve-year-old helped me appreciate. It's not the meme that's funny all by itself; it's the meme viewed against the background of a whole series of thematic variations. It's like this with knock-knock jokes too, or lightbulb jokes. Part of what makes the joke funny is the appreciation that it is a variation on a theme. The joke is at once a move inside a genre and a comment on it, and understanding the joke is really a sensitivity to a whole swath of shared life, background assumptions, images, self-images, and so on. This is just the same sort of ironic self-reference that you see everywhere you look in the history of art, in pop music, in pop culture such as television sitcoms, and now in a novel form, the internet meme.

Memes really are always about appropriation. Memes work with theft over honest toil—or rather, they toil to sample, copy, rip off, and in doing so to be funny and smart.

This is one reason why young folk in "the memery" the world over balked at the 2016 decision to add Pepe the Frog to the Anti-Defamation League's hate symbols list (at least at the time). To them the idea that Pepe is a symbol of the new racist right wing is about as dumb as the idea that Queen Elizabeth, whose disfigured image appeared so prominently in the sights and sounds of early punk rock, was a symbol *of* punk or anarchy. The punks used her, commented on her, dissed her, and in doing so they managed in a weird way to brand her as a punk grapheme. But even the least bit of fluency or cultural literacy would prevent anyone from thinking the queen was a punk rock icon in the relevant sense. And so with Pepe. The fact that some right-wing dingbats use this image in their internet social space doesn't make it theirs. Which is not to say that tides can't turn, fashions shift, and trends lead to one particular reading of Pepe gaining traction. It also doesn't mean that some uses of the image may not be straightforwardly anti-Semitic or hurtful (of course they can be). Nor is there any reason *not* to judge a politician—Trump, for example—for using Pepe for his own political ends. After all, Trump used Pepe precisely in the service of hate, not innocently. But the point remains, so kids everywhere would argue if pressed, that it is the very nature of the distinctive style of irony characteristic of this sort of appropriation that the dirt doesn't stick.

So Pepe, according to the memesters, is no swastika. Pepe isn't a symbol or an icon but a prop in a joke, and it is the joke that is offensive, not the prop. The swastika itself is different kind of case. Even the fact that it began as a backward form of an Indian religious symbol does nothing to prevent its being the case that it is now and forevermore a symbol of National Socialism.

The new memes aren't really new, no more so than jokes or irony. But the manner of transmission is new, as is the way in which whole collectives of people who've never met each other can organize and reorganize themselves into in-groups and audiences. And so it isn't surprising that there are now philosophers such as Simon Evnine at the University of Miami doing philosophy with, in, and about memes, and also young scholars such as Elizabeth Cantalamessa, also at the University of Miami, who sees in "memestreams" new possibilities for political investigation and what we might call alt-left and alt-feminist creativity.

# 45 | ADELE IN THE GOLDILOCKS ZONE

Pop singer Adele won six Grammy Awards for her album *21*. People like this music. And I can appreciate why. She nails it like a gymnast nails a landing. She gives us what we want to hear. Not too hot. Not too cold. Just right.

Music is a lot like clothing. We like our jeans pre-worn. When it comes to music, we like the novel to be familiar. That is, we like familiar varieties of *un*familiarity; we like things we've never heard before that sound like things we have heard before. If the music is too familiar, it's dull. But if it is *genuinely* new, if it really is novel, then it is obnoxious or—worst of all—not even recognizable as music at all.

We are attracted to music in the Goldilocks zone, as it has been called. And it is this that explains a familiar but nonetheless re-markable fact about musical style—namely, that styles change, and that therefore music has a history (a question I took up in Chapter 37). You can tell where and when a song was written, just by the sound of it. Why should that be? Is it that we have changed? Have the scope and reach of our emotional or cognitive lives changed? What is truly astonishing, when you stop to think about it, is that laws of style seem to circumscribe what any artist can hope to accomplish. However original, however diverse its influences, the art we produce bears not only our individual mark but that of the time and place where it originates.

The fact that style has a history makes sense given the drive for the familiar unfamiliar. It is the yearning for the unfamiliar that propels us toward change, and so in the direction of the new; it is the lust after characteristically familiar forms of novelty that keeps us safely in the comfort zone set up by our local horizon. Music, from this standpoint, is a conversation that elapses in time. We are done with what's been said, but not interested in just any old thing that might be sayable, only in what is pertinent to current concerns. As the musical conversation unfolds over time our expectations and interests change, and so the invisible shows up, the new gets old, and the old acquires the comfort and the emotional value of, say, an old sweater. (Some old sweaters are cherished; we give others away, and throw some out.)

The thing to notice is that it isn't as though we don't *like* novel music. It's that we don't even hear it; we are deaf to its musical ideas. The encounter with genuinely novel music is like hearing a conversation in a language we don't know. This is why music that is now canonical and tame for us—Stravinsky's *Rite of Spring*, for example—could once have caused audiences to riot and storm out of the hall. The music hasn't changed, but we have.

According to scientists interviewed for a 2012 article in the *Wall Street Journal*, music with certain properties—roughly, music that occupies the Goldilocks zone—sets up the release of dopamine in reward circuitry in the brain.[1] No doubt. But it would be a mistake to think this is why we like the music. It is rather that we get dopamine release *because* we enjoy the music, because we are sensitive to the way it fits into and plays against a musical conversation, which is really to say a whole musical culture. The same music, but in a different musical context, won't have those same effects, and primarily because it won't interest us.

Stravinsky wasn't in the business of selling records and winning Grammy Awards. He wasn't serving likes and dislikes; he was doing something very different. It is a challenge to say just what. Perhaps he was investigating the limits of music itself as a mode of musical expression. Far from trying to please, he was looking into the nature of music as a domain for meaningful activity at all. Not so Adele. For now at least, she's happy to give us what we want. Neuroscience helps us see how Adele can serve up a Happy Meal but not how her music can manage to be a thing of lasting value. To understand that, we need to look elsewhere.

# 46 | MIND IN THE NATURAL WORLD: CAN PHYSICS EXPLAIN IT?

Carlo Rovelli's *Seven Brief Lessons on Physics,* originally published as a series of essays in an Italian newspaper, is a very clear book, and it is likely to provoke in readers, as it provoked in me, a desire to learn more about space, time, quantum reality, the nature of gravity, our universe, and, finally, ourselves.[1] I read the book by the noted physicist in a single sitting with pleasure and mounting excitement.

*Seven Brief Lessons* does not shy away from philosophy, and it is an admirable testament, I think, to the fact that philosophy and natural science, although perhaps never one and the same, must grapple with each other.

None of Rovelli's "lessons" left me satisfied, but I mean this in a good way. They all left me wanting more. For example, when the author explains that the "earth does not turn around [the sun] because of a mysterious force [gravity] but because it is racing directly in a space that inclines, like a marble that rolls in a funnel," I found myself wishing he would then cash out this funnel metaphor in a way that doesn't take gravity for granted (15). This is less a criticism than an appreciation that this lovely little book, which

I shared with my eleven-year-old, is as much an expression of curiosity as it is an attempt to set out the answers.

On one point, though, I think the book deserves to be challenged more forcefully.

If you open the neck of a balloon, the balloon will shoot hither and thither; it is impossible to say where it will land. This is not, the author rightly points out, because the action of the released balloon is truly random but simply because we, given our knowledge (or, as he puts it, "the limited sets of properties [of the balloon] with which we interact" (64), are unable to predict which way the balloon will travel. In contrast, he suggests, an all-knowing or supersensible creature would be able simply to see what the balloon was going to do when its neck was opened, for such an all-knower would directly appreciate the exact positions of the molecules within the balloon and out of which it is composed. Such a superintelligent being would perceive that there is no balloon, that there are only atoms obeying entirely fixed, independent laws of nature, laws that it is in a position to comprehend.

The same point can be made, argues Rovelli, about time. Time seems to flow. There seems to be before and after, past, present, and future. But this, as with the balloon, is an illusion that is produced in us as a result of our parochial limitations—that is, because of the "profoundly relational nature of the concepts we use to organize the world." He explains:

> For a hypothetically super-sensible being, there would be no
> "flowing" of time: the universe would be a single block of
> past, present, and future. But due to the limitations of our

consciousness we perceive only a blurred vision of the world
and live in time. (69)

But we must ask: are there not phenomena whose essential *irreversibility* seems to require of us that we think of them as unfolding in time, that is, as captured by time's flow?

Even if we grant that statistical thermodynamics can explain why heat dissipates and chicks don't turn into eggs (as Rovelli explains), one can wonder whether we can make sense of the phenomenon of consciousness itself without time. Melodies, for example, are creatures of time, and does it make any sense to imagine that one might *think* backward?

Which leads me to wonder: Would Rovelli's supersensible being, far from having discovered the unreality of time and balloons, be rather in the position of one who could not think and who was deaf to music?

Rovelli, whose book is not dogmatic, appreciates that consciousness is still poorly understood. (He speaks of "limitations of consciousness" in the quotation given earlier.) Moreover, he says: "In the big picture of contemporary science, there are many things that we do not understand, and one of the things that we understand least about is ourselves." (73)

He is also admirably insistent that science has no business overlooking or ignoring this question: "I've set out to show how the world looks in the light of science, and we are part of that world, too." (73)

But Rovelli remains hopeful; I worry that his hopefulness is misplaced.

The scientific picture of the world, Rovelli says, lives within us, in the space of our thoughts, and our relation to the world is constrained by our ignorance, our senses, our intelligence. But these limitations, he insists, are not fixed. They are set by the "mental evolution of our species and are in continuous evolution." (68) Moreover, he believes, our knowledge, such as it is, frequently reflects the world as it really is, in itself. There really was a Big Bang. We really have come to understand the fabric of space. And, in part, this is because we "learn to gradually change our conceptual framework and to adapt it to what we learn." (68)

But who is this "we" that succeeds in modifying the very limitations of our relation to the world around us? And is there some reason, beyond a brute optimism, for thinking that evolution, a natural process itself, would have the effect of letting us, as he puts it, get it right and find what we are seeking?

Rovelli wants to resist the thought that we somehow stand outside of nature when we describe it. We, like everything else, are in continuous transaction with the world around us. We carry information about the world in our brains, just as a raindrop carries information about the presence of a cloud in the sky and a footprint carries information about the one who made it. But the raindrop and the footprint, for all they are packed with information, have no knowledge. Why think the brain is any different?

Rovelli seems to appreciate this unbridged gulf, for he resorts to highly poetic language when he addresses exactly this issue: "The primal substance of our thought is an extremely rich gathering of information that's accumulated, exchanged, and continually elaborated." (70) Indeed! But neither Rovelli nor anyone else has yet explained how that process of continual elaboration is a physical process or how it is a process unfolding in our brains.

Rovelli's is a beautiful book and I recommend it. But I warn the reader, and I warn Rovelli himself: if he is right that we belong to the very same nature it is the project of physics to understand, then it may be that there is something incomplete or not yet adequate in our physics itself. For we have nothing like an adequate account of ourselves in the natural world.

# 47 | ART AT THE LIMITS OF NEUROSCIENCE

I should say up front that it is not my aim to say no to neuroscience. I have no desire whatsoever to do so.[1]

My aim rather is to say yes to art. My concern, at bottom, is that neuroscience does not have the resources to say yes to art; it cannot bring art into focus.

Here's why.

Neuroscientists working on art almost universally assume what I call the trigger conception of art. According to the trigger conception, artworks are stimuli that trigger a special kind of event—the aesthetic experience—in us.

But aesthetic experiences are not triggered in us. And artworks are not triggers.

As to the first point, artworks do not trigger aesthetic experiences because aesthetic experiences are not episodes in consciousness like sensory episodes that start and stop anchored in exposure to a stimulus. In a sense, they are not *experiences* as the term is used in consciousness research and philosophy. They are less like headaches or perceptual episodes and more like patterns of curiosity, interest, or caring. An aesthetic experience isn't the sort of thing that happens once and for all—when does your aesthetic experience of a poem come to an end? when you've stopped looking at the page?—and for the same reason that one's concern for a political cause, or interest in a person, doesn't happen, at a moment, once and for all.

Aesthetic experience, insofar as it is a phenomenon at all, is *critical*—that is, it unfurls in a space of thought and talk, a space of criticism, and so, in an important sense, in a shared communicative space; aesthetic experiences are not private or individual but social. Finding the words to articulate your aesthetic response is itself a creative act, and usually also an emotional one; it is not something we typically do on our own, individually, simply in one-on-one response to an artwork, thought of as a sort of stimulus atom. We strive to have aesthetic experience, and we do so as members of a culture, and in particular as members of an art culture.

So there is no fixed datum, the aesthetic experience, that occurs in the individual and that can be studied using the methods of psychophysics or brain imaging or other such means of neural analysis. Aesthetic experience is something persons, not brains, undertake, and they do so always in the setting of others and against the background of a culture and a history.

None of this is likely to be very surprising to those who are with me in insisting that we say yes to art.

And of course none of this is to deny that you can study what happens in the brain when we do all the different things we do when we are aesthetically engaged with artworks, such as looking, listening, thinking, arguing, describing, associating, learning, reading, arguing, et cetera.

But there is unlikely to be any interesting unity among the neural substrates of aesthetic experience. Such a structure of looking, listening, thinking, reading, arguing, and remembering, distributed as it may be in time, is just too disunited to have a plausible, *interesting* neural correlate. And anyway, even if there is something that seems to gel at the neural level and jump out as a candidate for the neural correlate of aesthetic experience, it is unlikely that it will shed any light at all on the aesthetic experience itself. How can information about what is going on in my nervous system, unfolding beneath awareness, on the time scale of milliseconds, be usefully informative as to the whole person, socially embedded participation in a practice of looking, thinking, feeling, reflecting, and evaluating? How can it bear on the art, or on what deserves to be called aesthetic experience?

You might, on behalf of neuroscience, be tempted to adopt a divide-and-conquer strategy. Granted, you might concede, we can't bring aesthetic experience itself, whatever that is, into focus in the lab, but we can look at something simpler but related, such as preference judgments or reports about whether we find a stimulus "moving."[2]

There are roughly three problems with this kind of approach.

First, liking something or finding it moving isn't the same as finding it aesthetically significant. I may not like art that I value, and merely liking something is not enough to value it aesthetically. I may not be moved by a work I value, and I may be moved by work I don't value. Interestingly, I might find a single work moving sometimes but not at other times. I might learn to find it moving or come to find it no longer moving.

Second, insofar as we can collect data on preference or "movingness," or vividness of imagery or whatever, insofar as these really become fixed points whose meaning is secure, then this is probably because we have stepped outside the domain of the aesthetic. I say this because I think of a liking-response to a work of art not as *the* aesthetic experience or judgment or evaluation itself but rather as one moment, maybe just the initiation, of the relevant aesthetic encounter. There's the initial liking (or disliking), and then there's the accounting for one's response. Finding the words to explain or justify or make sense of the response sometimes also has the effect of changing our response. To separate isolated responses or judgments about liking or emotional power or lovingness or vividness or whatever from the conversations and investigations and work of bringing the artwork into focus for further reflection is to give up the aesthetic.

You might object that this is unfair to neuroaesthetics, for neuroscience is forced to simplify, to detach aspects and parts in order to get an experimental purchase on the phenomenon. I appreciate this response. But this awkward impasse is the consequence, I think, of insisting on saying yes to art. It is false to the phenomenon of art in our lives to pretend that liking-responses and suchlike, on their own, can go proxy, in however limited a way, for art or aesthetic meaning.

All this is related to the fact that what "liking" or "finding something moving" means, in an art context, is up for grabs. Is On Kawara moving, or Sol LeWitt? The very meaning of the term *moving* needs to be reinvented if we are to ask the question seriously in reference to these artists. We certainly can't assume any freestanding metric for making evaluations or comparisons among artists. One way to bring this out: When we respond to an artwork seriously by expressing our love of it, or how moving we find it, or how vividly we experience its images, we are not employing external, artist- or content-neutral terms of appraisal or expressions of feeling. Rather, we are engaging with the artwork on its own terms, *inside* the space it opens up.

So the trigger conception is mistaken insofar it takes for granted that aesthetic experiences are timeable, operationalizable, stable episodes in consciousness that occur inside individuals.

But it is also misguided in the way it thinks of the artwork—namely, as something that supposedly triggers. (This the third problem.)

No doubt, insofar as the artwork is a material or concrete entity—insofar as it is a song, or a sculpture, or a painting—then it will be liable to trigger perceptual (or emotional, or kinesthetic, or empathetic) responses in perceivers. But that's true of any old thing and has nothing distinctively to do with its status as an artwork. A Mondrian will activate color areas in the brain, and a dance may activate systems required for action perception, but so will a colorful ad in the newspaper or a glimpse of the crush of passengers during the morning commute, respectively. Insofar as works of art are perceptible, then our experience of them depends on the exercise of our perceptual capacities, and so it depends in turn on the activation of the neural substrates necessary for such exercise. But to see the Mondrian is not merely to see a colorful surface, and to see the dance is not merely to perceive moving people. The art in these things consists not in some further disposition to trigger a response, neurological or otherwise, but rather in the ways these works provide us the opportunity to react, think, look, judge, and also catch ourselves in the act of thus reacting, thinking, looking, and judging. *The work of art is not a trigger. It is an opportunity.*

One upshot of this is that although all art is specific, concrete, material, what differentiates works of art from any other item of human manufacture or technology, from other artifacts, is what I will call, in an admittedly non-standard use of this term, its logical standing. As an example of what I have in mind: The model unit in an apartment complex may be physically identical to any one of the homes, but it is a different kind of thing. It is a display, a thing for show, a model. The same is true, I think, of works of art. The artwork may be a picture, but it no more functions as a picture than the model unit functions as a home; similarly, a choreographic work, however much it looks like dancing, is never just dancing. Art plays a different, logical role, as opposed to a practical or functional one.

There is in fact a very simple marker of this distinct art role. When human makings are put to work logically or rhetorically as art, we can never rely on any prior or independent standards when it comes to making sense of them or evaluating them.

If you define neuroaesthetics as the use of neuroscience to explain art and aesthetic experience, then it is not surprising that neuroaesthetics fails: art just isn't a phenomenon (neurological or experiential) to be explained by neuroscience, psychology, or any other empirical science; it is, rather, a mode of questioning and inquiry. As James Baldwin believed, art aims to uncover the questions that have been occluded by the answers.[3] And this is because, in a way, art is philosophy.

But maybe we can rethink the meaning of neuroaesthetics. This alternative conception would start with the dual propositions that art aims at a distinct kind of understanding, something like philosophical understanding, and that neuroscience, for its part, is less the name of a settled discipline whose standards of success and failure are already quite clear, but rather denotes the attempt to frame, as we have until now been unable to frame, a plausible bio-logical conception of what it is to be human. Neuroscience, on such a conception, comprises philosophy. Neuroaesthetics, then, can be our term for the project of looking to art for a better insight into what it is to be human. On this way of thinking, neuroaesthetics is not the application of neuroscience to art; it is, or might be-come, the turning to art as a resource for helping us work toward a more adequate neuroscience, that is, a more adequate conception of ourselves.[4]

# NOTES

## CHAPTER 1

1. Blake Gopnik, "32 Short Thoughts About Andy Warhol's Campbell's Soup Can Paintings at MoMA," *Artnet*, October 9, 2015, https://news.artnet. com/exhibitions/andy-warhols-campbells-soup-can-paintings-at-moma-338874.

2. Alva Noë, *Strange Tools: Art and Human Nature* (New York: Hill and Wang/FSG, 2015.

## CHAPTER 8

1. Oscar Wilde, *The Decay of Lying in Intentions* (1891).

## CHAPTER 18

1. Anne Hollander, *Seeing through Clothes* (New York: Viking, 1978).

## CHAPTER 19

1. See my *Out of Our Heads* (Hill and Wang/FSG, 2009) for a discussion of this topic.

## CHAPTER 21

1. This quote is taken from Michael Fried's beautiful book Menzel's Realism: *Art and Embodiment in Nineteenth-Century Berlin* (Yale University Press, 2002).

## CHAPTER 23

1. Roger Ebert, "Why I Hate 3D Movies," *Newsweek (online),* May 9, 2010.

2. See, for example, Dennett's *Consciousness Explained* (Boston: Little Brown, 1991).

## CHAPTER 24

1. Mori's original discussion was published in a Japanese journal called *Energy* in 1970. It is available online at spectrum.ieee.org.
2. See Lawrence Weschler, *The Uncanny Valley: Adventures in Narrative* (New York: Counterpoint, 2012).
3. Brian Selznick, *The Invention of Hugo Cabret* (New York: Scholastic, 2007).

## CHAPTER 30

1. Michael Fried, "Art and Objecthood," in his *Art and Objecthood* (University of Chicago, 1998), 148–172.
2. See Blake Gopnik, "Rembrandt's Genius Lies in the Brand, Not the Hand," *The New York Times*, November 2, 2013. See also "In Defense of Faking It," which replies to my criticisms here, in *Bending Concepts: The Held Essays on Visual Art 2011–2017.*
3. Stanley Cavell, "On Aesthetic Problems of Modern Philosophy," in *Must We Mean What We Say* (Cambridge: Cambridge University Press, 1969).
4. Peter Schjeldahl, "Fakery," *The New Yorker*, November 8, 2013.
5. John Dewey, *Art as Experience* (London: Penguin, 1934).
6. Myer Schapiro, "On Perfection, Coherence, and Unity of Form and Content," in *Theory and Philosophy of Art: Style, Artist, and Society* (George Braziller, 1994).

## CHAPTER 31

1. See Alexander Nagel, *Bending Concepts: The Held Essays on Visual Art 2011–2017* (Rail Editions, 2019).

## CHAPTER 32

1. See Alexander Nagel, "Beyond the Relic Cult of Art," in *Bending Concepts: The Held Essays on Visual Art 2011–2017* (Rail Editions, 2019).

## CHAPTER 33

1. Benjamin Binstock, *Vermeer's Family Secrets: Genius, Discovery, and the Unknown Apprentice* (New York: Routledge, 2008), 281.

## CHAPTER 34

1. See Gopnik's contribution to *Bending Concepts: The Held Essays on Visual Art 2011–2017* (Rail Editions, 2019).
2. Peter Scheldahl, "Faker," *The New Yorker*, November 8, 2013.
3. See Schapiro, "On Perfection, Coherence, and Unity of Form and Content," in *Theory and Philosophy of Art: Style, Artist, and Society* (George Braziller, 1994).

## CHAPTER 36

1. Richard O Prum, *The Evolution of Beauty* (Doubleday, 2017), 27.

## CHAPTER 37

1. S. Pinker, *How the Mind Works* (New York: W. W. Norton, 1997).
2. Gary Marcus, *Guitar Zero: The Science of Becoming Musical at Any Age* (Penguin, 2012).

## CHAPTER 39

1. Matt Trueman, "Beyoncé Accused of 'Stealing' Dance Moves in New Video," *The Guardian*, October 10, 2011.

## CHAPTER 40

1. Hilton Als, "Postscript: David Bowie, 1947–2016," *The New Yorker*, January 11, 2016.
2. Ben Ratliff, "Listening to David Bowie: A Critic's Tour of His Musical Changes," *The New York Times,* January 11, 2016.
3. Here: Ben Ratliff, review of Kurt Cobain, "Montage of Heck: The Home Recordings," *The New York Times*, November 18, 2015.
4. Simon Critchley, "Nothing Remains: David Bowie's Vision of Love," *The New York Times*, January 11, 2016.

## CHAPTER 41

1. Hubert Dreyfus and Sean Dorrance Kelly, *All Things Shining: Reading the Western Classics to Find Meaning in a Secular Age* (Free Press, 2011).
2. Stephen Hawking and Leonard Mlodinov, *The Grand Design* (Bantam, 2012).

## CHAPTER 42

1. Guy Deutscher, *The Unfolding of Language* (Holt, 2006).

## CHAPTER 45

1. Michaeleen Doucleff, "Anatomy of a Tear-Jerker," *The Wall Street Journal*, February 11, 2012.

## CHAPTER 46

1. New York: Riverhead, 2016.

## CHAPTER 47

1. This is a shortened version of the text of a lecture presented at the Volksbühne in Berlin on September 28, 2018, at the tenth annual meeting of the Society for Neuroaesthetics.
2. This is the strategy pursued by G. Gabrielle Starr and the neuroscientist Ed Vessell. See Starr's book *Feeling Beauty: The Neuroscience of Aesthetic Experience* (MIT, 2013).
3. See James Baldwin, "The Creative Process," in *Baldwin: Collected Essays*, edited by Toni Morrison (New York: The Library of America, 1998).
4. Thanks to co-panelists in Berlin, for valuable discussion, especially: Elena Agudio, Joerg Fingerhut, Beatriz Calvo-Merino, Warren Neidich, Alexandra Pirici, and Ed Vessel. Thanks also to Talbot Brewer, Garnett Cadogan, Matthew B. Crawford, and Joseph E. Davis, at the Institute for Advanced Studies in Culture at the University of Virginia, where I had a chance to present a version of this talk at February 2020.

# ACKNOWLEDGMENTS

Thanks to my friends at the 13.7 Project at NPR—especially Adam Franks and Wright Bryan—for the opportunity to do this work. Blake Gopnik and Alexander Nagel are mentioned throughout these pages, and they are due many thanks. I have had them in mind throughout. I am grateful to my family, friends, and students for their love and for the inspiration they provide.

A note on sources and permissions: The writings collected here rework material originally published at NPR's *13.7: Cosmos and Culture* (www.npr.org/13.7) and are reproduced here with permission, except for the following.

"Art Placebo" was published in winter 2013 in *The Brooklyn Rail* as one of the Held Essays on Visual Art. It appears, with the other contributions to this series, in *Bending Concepts: The Held Essays on Visual Art, 2011–2017* (New York: Rail Editions, 2019). I am grateful for the permission to reprint this essay here.

"The Performance Art of David Bowie: A Remembrance" and "Art at the Limits of Neuroscience" have not been previously published.

# INDEX

For the benefit of digital users, indexed terms that span two pages (e.g., 52–53) may, on occasion, appear on only one of those pages.